# LIVING THE GOOD FIGHT

# LIVING THE GOOD FIGHT

## A Mother's Journey of Faith, Hope and AML Leukemia

TRACY KEARCHER

XULON PRESS

Xulon Press
2301 Lucien Way #415
Maitland, FL 32751
407.339.4217
www.xulonpress.com

Paperback ISBN-13: 978-1-66282-521-7
Ebook ISBN-13: 978-1-66282-522-4

To my sister, Amanda, and our **Perfect** Stem Cell Match
To my parents, Marilyn and Joseph, who were always
by my side, and to Tim, Alyssa, and Mr. Matt, who
I fought for each and every day

"Those who trust in the Lord will find new strength.
They will soar high on wings like eagles.
They will run and not grow weary.
They will walk and not faint."
Isaiah 40:31

# TABLE OF CONTENTS

# INTRODUCTION

Being an oncology nurse gives you a perspective on life that most people don't understand. For my entire career, I have provided care and treatment to people who are on the edge of life. There are a wide range of emotions and losses that come from a diagnosis of cancer. The loss of a "normal life" and the acceptance of a "new normal" is one of the hardest.

I have had countless profound and meaningful conversations with patients over the years, listening, learning, and growing from each experience along the way. All the knowledge, training, and years of hard work make family and strangers alike turn to you with questions you have answers to but may not want to share. When my cousin Tracy was in the emergency room and I heard of the tests that were being ordered, I knew what the medical team was looking for. Cancer. More specifically, leukemia.

I am very happy to say that this is Tracy's story and one she is able to tell herself. I thank the hematology team who cared for her, the research that has brought treatments that have improved patient outcomes, the support of her family, and her sheer perseverance for her survival. I am also proud that Tracy is brave enough to share her post-treatment story. Of course, all cancer survivors are grateful to be alive, but the ramifications of treatment and complications can wreak havoc on their daily lives. Open and honest conversations and acknowledgment of their struggles can be a lifeline when things seem unbearable. I'm confident Tracy's story will be relatable to many, and hopefully it will help others with their healing process.

Cheryl Walsh (Gans),
former chemotherapy resource nurse and bone marrow transplant nurse at Yale New Haven Hospital, New Haven, CT

# IT'S COMING

March 18, 2017
My body is rebelling against me.

t's aching and I am sweating on and off; I can't seem to warm up. Tim places his hand on mine after turning the heat to full blast. Surely now I will warm up. My teeth are chattering uncontrollably. I can't stop them no matter how much I try. My body feels so cold; it's freezing in this car. I am covered in a blanket with my eyes closed, and the only sound I hear is the noise of my upper teeth forcefully making contact with my lower jaw. The noise normally left my nerves rattled, but today it is the least of my concerns.

The car swerves abruptly. I press my hands against the side of the seat to steady myself and tell myself to breathe. The only other time in my life when I saw Tim so nervous was when our daughter, Alyssa, was coming. Watch out, world! Tim had precious cargo in the car and was coming through.

Now he's gritting his teeth and I can see the tension in his jaw as he drives like a crazy man trying to get us to Hartford Hospital. Heaven forbid we get stuck behind someone going five miles below the speed limit. Tim takes bad driving as a personal insult from others, while I try to tell him that everyone has a story: maybe their wife was just diagnosed with cancer, or maybe they are late for work and if they don't make it in on time they will be let go.

Today I say nothing, as the pain has taken my voice. I'm actually happy he's driving like we're in the Daytona 500. My mouth has been throbbing for the past week, ever since I had a pesky wisdom tooth extracted. At times I thought I was over the discomfort, but then the pain reemerged. To complicate things further, eating solid food worsened the pain so I resorted to drinking protein smoothies. After a week of the smoothie diet, I've lost four pounds and have absolutely no energy. Last weekend, when I was sorting Girl Scout Cookies for our Daisy troop, I became completely winded and had to sit down a few times. Whatever's causing this tooth infection sure is strong.

My dentist was perplexed, as the heavy-duty antibiotics he prescribed a few days ago should have helped me feel better by now. The crater from where the tooth had been didn't appear to be infected, so why is my mouth causing me such pain? Hopefully, they'll figure it all out at the hospital. I just need to close my eyes and take deep breaths. I'm praying the oral surgeons have answers to help me feel better soon; however, I feel myself getting worse by the moment. Something's terribly wrong.

Luckily, this late Saturday morning, the day after St. Patrick's Day, the traffic is light. As we arrive at Hartford Hospital and enter the emergency room, Tim guides me in. There's a disconnect between my mind and my body's actions; my thoughts are fuzzy and I can't seem to focus. Something very strange is going on. This is one heck of a wisdom tooth infection.

# STORM WARNING

A few minor signs popped up here and there. My regular workout DVDs were kicking my butt more than usual, and this was just the warm-up. Walking up my basement stairs left me winded and out of breath. During the night I sweated profusely, and it soaked through my pajamas. What was going on? I knew I wasn't pregnant.

With the two young kids, I didn't have time to dwell on the symptoms. Like every other mom, I kept up the crazy pace of being a stay-at-home mom.

Then I got a very painful infection following a wisdom tooth extraction. Two weeks of drinking protein smoothies, visiting the dentist multiple times, and babying my mouth did nothing. I felt worse and found myself devoid of all energy. My husband drove quickly to the nearest emergency room while my parents watched the kids.

It was a late Saturday morning. The pain was unbearable, and I shivered uncontrollably as the emergency room nurses performed the intake questionnaire and examination. Finally, the oral surgeon and nurses were called in to run lab work and do a full evaluation.

The pain medication took the edge off as they examined my mouth. Good news! The infection was mild. The wound was beginning to heal. So why did I feel so miserable?

The doctor announced that my blood levels were elevated and off. It must be anemia again, I thought to myself. I was anemic as a teenager. Maybe it was back? Relieved, I mentally ran through the simple fix: eat more steaks and spinach and begin taking an iron supplement again. I knew constipation would result, but it could be worse. Just a few hours later, it was. The night shift nurse and doctor dropped the "L" word.

It's vivid in my memory. My sister Amanda arrived so Tim could go home to situate and settle the kids. Our brains couldn't process the "L" word; we looked at each other with disbelief. The doctor left before we uttered a word, probably thinking it best to give us a moment. She did mention that a bone marrow biopsy was the next step before leaving the room. It would pinpoint the strain, but it was indeed leukemia.

We looked at each other and said at the same time, "Holy crap! Did she just say leukemia?"

The next day, I awoke in my hospital bed for the very first time. My hematologist made his rounds at the crack of dawn. I quickly learned that he was well known for making his rounds early and then spending the rest of his busy day in his office. I also had a hematologist because I had blood cancer. It was all so much, too much, to take in. Black ominous clouds came rolling in. My night had been full of unfamiliar voices, loud beeping noises, and the grave sensation of being hooked up to all sorts of IVs. I was anything but well rested. Little did I know that this was my new normal. Sleeping straight through the night was a novelty that slipped into the past.

As I was waking up and trying to adjust to this foreign feeling of being in a hospital room, Tim was on his way to visit me for the first time since I'd been moved to the oncology floor. The nurse wheeled my bed past the "Helen & Harry Gray Cancer Center" sign, and I wanted to scream out in horror and get violently ill at the exact same time. I was entering "Cancer Land." Just the word *cancer* was (and is) traumatic. Throughout my life, I'd known loved ones with various cancers, some of whom had perished from them. As I tried to process my diagnosis, my few experiences with cancer flooded my memory.

One of my mother's best friends, my Confirmation sponsor, died from cancer when I was a teenager. I went to the hospital to say goodbye to her. As I walked into her room, I instantly noticed her yellow skin tone and her bloated, puffy cheeks. The many medications she was on had created havoc in her body.

This was not the radiant Jeanie I had known growing up. Cancer was torturing her. Breaking her apart piece by piece. It simply wasn't fair. After an unsuccessful marriage and experiencing a great deal of pain, she was finally happily remarried with a teenage daughter who desperately needed her mother. My thoughts jerked me back to the present. My two little ones needed me too. We lost Jeanie and I didn't understand why or how God could take her away from us. It wasn't fair; it didn't make sense. My diagnosis lingered in the air of my room, and I couldn't believe or process it yet. I came in yesterday for a silly tooth infection. They must have mixed up the lab work. I had a family to raise and a special-needs son to attend to. My kids needed me. I didn't want to suffer.

Tim had heard some of the discussion through Amanda and was in shock as well. During his ride from Ellington to Hartford that morning, he did his best to be optimistic about my condition and told himself that there was no way I had leukemia. I was the same woman who had kicked his butt in the Litchfield Road Race, passing him out at mile five. I was completely healthy a month ago.

He entered the hospital on the chilly late-winter morning and took the elevator up to the fourth floor. He quickly recognized a familiar face that happened to be at the nurses' station when he stepped off the elevator. The doctor who treated me the prior day in the emergency room was now working the morning shift and was talking with one of the nurses. When she glanced up and her eyes met his, to Tim's surprise, her facial expression immediately changed. She tensed up and no longer wore the smile she just had when conversing with her coworker; instead, she appeared quite serious and concerned.

The sudden change in mood was followed by a slight nod as Tim passed by. *What could this mean?* Tim thought. *Why did she look so concerned?* Little did Tim know that those few seconds from when he stepped off the elevator would be ingrained in his memory forever. More than he could possibly know was said at that moment without anyone saying a word. As his mind raced and his feet carried him down the hall, he arrived in my new "home" to see the lights off. The hematologist was setting the stage for our road ahead. Nothing prepares you for this kind of conversation.

There are no classes in school or advice from family and friends on how to deal with being told your wife and children's mother has blood cancer. This subject is so heinous, we don't even consider talking about it in fear that it may jeopardize our future or lead to bad omens. With so much beauty in our surroundings and experiences on earth, why spend time dwelling on the negative? Well, there Tim was, with little time to prepare for this crossroads in his life. Even if there were more time, he knew he wouldn't have been in any better condition to receive the news. The doctor began to share the specifics of my diagnosis, the possible paths of treatment, and the grave situation I was in.

Receiving this type of news tears down barriers we have in controlling our emotions. The pain and hurt comes out like a tidal wave that's been released from places inside of us, ones we don't even know existed. The room starts spinning and your mind tries to focus on something else to keep from drifting back into the dark, deep abyss. After a while, Tim no longer heard the words coming out of the oncologist's month. He'd heard enough to know that his wife's life was in jeopardy.

I never left Hartford Hospital. I never had a chance to say goodbye to my kids, pack their lunches one last time, or arrange for carpools. My life's fate was out of my hands. Less than twenty-four hours after being admitted to the hospital, I was undergoing induction chemotherapy. I learned quickly: this was the first step for any acute leukemia treatment.

I was still in a state of complete shock. Tracy Lynn Kearcher had AML leukemia (acute myeloid), a form of blood cancer. Not only did I have leukemia, but two weeks into my stay after the first bone marrow biopsy (one of way too many) results came back, my family and I learned I had a strand of leukemia known as inversion of chromosome 3. This strand was overly aggressive and known to be resistant to chemotherapy. Talk about feeling doomed.

Acute myeloid leukemia (AML) is a rare form of cancer accounting for 1 percent of all cancers. It is an aggressive, rapidly progressing disease that requires invasive therapy. It is generally a disease of older people. It produces excessive immature white blood cells. This cancer usually starts in the bone marrow and spreads quickly throughout the blood. Patients with inv(3) show an extremely poor response to chemotherapy. Studies show a median survival rate of 10.3 months (Smol, Thomas 2014).

# WHEN EVERYTHING CHANGES

This isn't what they wanted for me.

was born on June 14, and as my close friends and family know, I love sharing my birthday with Flag Day. In elementary school, the special assembly for the flag felt like it could have been for me. How can this be happening to our family?

I am their first-born daughter and always felt well loved by my parents, Marilyn and Joseph Lipsky. While we did not have a huge home or go on extravagant vacations, my sister and I were always encouraged and cherished. My mom helped my sister and I with homework each and every night until algebra came along, and she had to pass the torch to my dad. To this day we are a close family—we celebrate every holiday together and have a yearly family summer vacation. When we were growing up, night after night, Amanda and I danced around the kitchen, singing along with Amy Grant as we took our time drying dishes, our nightly chore.

My dad loved to see us happy and healthy. He was our soccer coach for years. Even though he never played a game of soccer in his entire life, he watched every coaching video available to man so he could be the very best coach. Little did he know that years later that same determination would be spent researching the latest and greatest AML leukemia treatments for hours online. Searching for ways to support his green-eyed baby girl. He even offered to sell his most cherished possession, his *Josie Rose* (a boat he saved up for years to buy and named after my deceased grandmother and beloved great aunt).

Throughout my life he loved to fix anything and everything. If something broke, my dad could fix it. When I read the book *Mr. Fix-It* as a child, I just knew it was about my dad. I was convinced he could fix everything, even a broken heart. When I was diagnosed, it was the very first time in our lives that there was something my dad couldn't fix.

My mom has the biggest heart of anyone I know. Somehow, she managed to become my best friend and survive the dreaded teenage years while still ensuring my sister and I respected her authority. She could always tell how I was feeling by simply looking at my face. Now, when she looked at me in the eyes, she was overcome with grief and endless amounts of worry.

In an instant she went from not knowing what AML leukemia was to living it day in and day out for months. Her mind was on autopilot and our story spilled out unexpectedly at times. She found herself bearing her heart and soul at her parent-teacher conferences to other mothers: cherish your kids, you never know what tomorrow may bring.

What do you do when your entire existence is shaken? Every routine and relationship is impacted and forced onto a battlefield.

My parents could not have prepared for it, but they were determined to be the best caregivers humanly possible. They brought me into this world and were not going to let me leave it without a fight.

Every summer, my family and I vacationed in Wildwood, New Jersey. Some years my aunts and uncles along with my cousins joined us. My sister and I also got to bring a friend along on the trip. One year I remember every single lady in the house had their "monthly friend." My dad hid outside with his metal detector, shielded from all the hormones and ever-changing moods.

Each year the gang spent the week walking, reading, and gabbing along the shore. I spent hours reading tearjerker novels day after day. My mom saw tears streaming down my face and said, "Stop crying—what the heck are you reading?" I replied, "these stories are so beautiful. The way the characters cherish each moment on earth together and see the world in a different light than most people do. They have newfound values and such a strong faith in God. They live each day like it may be their last and never take life for granted. They were faced with the possibility of an untimely death."

Little did we know at that time, sitting in our beach chairs without a care in the world, that the characters in my book who were fighting a rare, aggressive form of cancer, or who were in remission, struggling to stay afloat mentally and physically, were a prelude to my future life.

After my diagnosis, I often wondered if we would ever vacation as a family at the Jersey Shore again. It was the place where I took some of my first steps, realized I love eating shrimp and lobster, and where Tim proposed on that beautiful July morning as the two of us sat all alone on the lifeguard stand, overlooking continuous blue skies. Our future was full of love and endless possibilities.

# IMPACT

Both sides of my family jumped into action. My in-laws moved into our house. They took care of the house and kids during the week so Tim could continue to work. My parents visited me each and every day at Hartford Hospital. Their day began at five a.m. so they could catch my doctor on his early rounds. One of them took notes, as we were constantly bombarded with new information and terminology now that we were living in Cancer Land.

Learning a new language is hard and we didn't have proper textbooks to refer to. My mom took a leave of absence from work while my dad, a computer network engineer, worked remotely from the hospital during the week. On weekends, my parents shifted their focus to the kids, so my sister and husband could take turns visiting me.

I had never been so scared in my entire life. Even though I did my best to stay positive and be an A+ patient, having my loved ones by my bedside most of the time was the greatest blessing a girl could ask for. As a chemotherapy patient, I was exhausted and overwhelmed by all the medical jargon being constantly thrown at me. It was reassuring to have my family present as I processed and digested the proposed treatment plans. My sister brought me crafting supplies and spring decorations for my hospital room; she became a regular at Michaels craft store. My husband brought a pile of the kids' schoolwork every time he came to the hospital. I loved to see their latest artwork and creativity. Looking at all the colors and glitter instantly cheered me up. He also took the time to frame family photos, so I remembered everything I had to fight for. Leukemia was certainly not my fault, but I always felt bad that everyone had to give up living their normal lives to be a part of saving mine.

I had a steady stream of friends and family who took time out of their busy lives to visit me in the hospital. They always say you can tell who your real friends are in times of trouble, and it's true. One of my best friends from college, Alaina, came to stay with me in the hospital. We laughed and cried, telling stories about the good old days. Our friendship had been a blessing to me throughout my life and her visit was just the medicine I needed. Many people walk into your life, but only true friends will drive five hours to stay with you in the hospital. The outpouring of support was truly amazing; friends I went to school with and hadn't talked to in years reached out to us. I felt surrounded by kindness, friendship, and support.

Meanwhile, it was decided to give me the highest dosage of chemotherapy possible due to my age, the severity of the leukemia strand, and my health preleukemia. The first round of chemotherapy is called induction chemotherapy. It's a combination of two types of chemotherapy: cytarabine and daunomycin. It has a 7 + 3 regimen, which means I received the cytarabine for a total of seven days and the daunomycin for the first three of the seven days. I was warned by my hematology doctor that I would not feel the nasty side effects until the following week. That was the week my hair fell out.

I was a hairdresser for over fifteen years and went to clients in the hospital to shave their hair after receiving a cancer diagnosis. I never thought it would be me having to have my head shaved. My mom and dad were in the room for moral support. A hairdresser and volunteer from the American Cancer Society shaved my hair for me. She swept into the room like a breath of fresh air full of positivity and encouragement. Having had her own battle with cancer at the age of nineteen, she openly shared her story. Her odds were bleak, like mine, but she stayed the course and fought just like I was fighting. She reminded me to keep taking it one step at a time, defying the odds one moment at a time. All these years later, I don't remember her name, but she was one of the many angels I met throughout my journey.

My days were filled with machines and testing. I became so weak that the nurses transported me to the different testing locations as I lay in my hospital bed. It felt like I was witnessing a never-ending sequence of fluorescent lights and caution signs as they pushed me along. I was in a maze of sterile hallways, fear, and loneliness.

Back in my room, multiple machines constantly monitored me. My heart rate, oxygen levels, blood pressure, body temperature, and bodily excrements were routinely measured and checked. Instead of having a morning cup of coffee, I was being poked for my daily blood work. This was my wake-up call every morning.

I had the pleasure of undergoing CAT scans, lung function tests, and ECGs to check on my organs to see how they were holding up throughout the chemotherapy treatment.

My room felt like a sound booth with a steady stream of beeping coming from the machines that surrounded me. I heard the beeping in my dreams. Thankfully, my family members took turns staying with me overnight at the hospital so I was never alone. Each one of them stated how it was impossible for them to get any sleep with all the noises and the routine vital checks throughout the night. It felt validating, and I longed for a night to sneak back into my own bed at home.

Chemotherapy wreaked havoc on my body. Its goal was to kill the cancer cells, but in the process, it destroyed healthy cells too. Cells in my intestinal lining, mouth, stomach, hair, and muscles were damaged and stripped away. Heartburn and acid reflux became part of my daily existence. If I could, I would've eaten Tums like candy. Unfortunately, the nurses had to monitor the amount. Vanilla Hoodsie Cups and red popsicles became my best friends, and daily nutrition. Everything else hurt my raw throat since my mucosa lining had been stripped away.

I rapidly lost weight and my body ached from simply lying in bed or sitting up in a chair all day, every day. My parents and Tim tried to get me to eat more by bringing in my favorite ice cream or milkshakes, but with all the chemotherapy and medications, everything tasted like metal. I didn't think it was possible, but chemotherapy even ruined my beloved Hunka Chunka PB Fudge sundae. All I tasted was cold metallic mush.

The nurses administered the chemotherapy through a port in my left arm. My left elbow could no longer bend—if I did mistakenly bend it, I'd pinch the line and cause my obnoxious machine to beep until the nurses came in to reset it. I was very careful to keep my IV site clean. Infection was one of the enemies I was constantly fighting against. There were a few times the site became red and hot to the touch. Thankfully, it healed and the port was never removed.

Meanwhile, the obnoxious machine was my buddy for over ten hours a day, for seven consecutive days. It was closer to me than my loved ones who took turns staying with me: it followed me to the bathroom, roamed the halls with me, and one day it even tried to take a shower with me. Luckily, the water was not turned on. I was a thirty-four-year-old mom who had run a half marathon and worked out daily. Overnight my life completely changed. I didn't know it at the time, but my life would never be the same.

As the chemotherapy progressed, my immune system was stripped away and I was unable to fight off any type of infection. My team of doctors cautioned me to stay away from fresh flowers and produce. I avoided anything that might have mold and bacteria on or in it. I could not eat any fresh fruit or raw vegetables; everything I ingested had to be fully cooked or processed. I fantasized about taking a nonmetallic bite into a fresh crunchy apple. I gazed longingly at my mom's salad like it was gold, envious of the luscious greens and crispy, crunchy vegetables. Day after day, I stared down plates full of overcooked mush. I felt like a caged animal. For the first and only time in my life, it was healthier and safer for me to eat canned Chef Boyardee than a salad with grilled chicken on it.

My mom and I have always been avid speed walkers throughout the years. Well, to this day, we could win an award for the most laps completed at Hartford Hospital's Helen & Harry Gray Cancer Center. Even if it was only one lap, my mom had me up and at 'em! I often would get sick take some time to settle and clean myself up. The next battle was trying to eat a few bites of food. Then, if I were up to it, we were off for another lap around the unit. Some days this little loop seemed like a piece of cake, while other days it felt like a marathon. The loop never changed, but my energy and strength sure did.

Throughout my entire leukemia battle, my parents were the captains of my cheerleading squad. They did their best to keep up a positive front. My mom even performed a private comedy hour for me when she tried to take up knitting again. YouTube's finest videos could not help her. At one point the needles were tossed into the trash can and she took off for an energetic stroll down the hallway to cool off.

I have never been one to sit still, but I was so tired from the che-motherapy. My eyes could not focus when I tried to pass the time by reading so I began to craft. Crafting was a great distraction, fun, and a way to release some of my nervous energy. I made barrettes and headbands and created a Facebook page, now called *Tracy Kearcher for a Cure*, where I posted my creations. Soon, friends, family, and strangers started to buy them. I donated one dollar from every sale to the Leukemia & Lymphoma Society. I was happy to donate to a cause that was now so near and dear to me, and it felt good to be making a difference, even though I desired to do it from a different location. A hair salon, Jack and Allies in Vernon and Rosenblatt's Clothing store all set up displays for me to sell my work. I will forever be grateful for their support. My mom and sister made the deliveries.

I also watched more television than I have ever watched in my entire life: HGTV, *The Golden Girls, Cake Boss, Chopped, Blue Bloods, Dirty Dancing, Rocky* and *Rocky II, III, IV,* and *V, Miracles from Heaven, Heaven Is for Real, God's Not Dead,* and many more. My daily television schedule featured where to turn for a good laugh. *The Golden Girls* kept me laughing with their witty humor and valuable life lessons. Sofia stated this about holding on to anger: "Anger is like a piece of shredded wheat stuck under your dentures. If you leave it there, you will get a blister. Then you will have to eat Jell-O for a whole week." At the time, I was eating a lot of Jell-O and this particular episode cracked me up. Laughter was the best distraction from the pain and constant stress of being ill, which was just what I needed.

# REMEMBERING SUN SHOWERS

All the hours facing the same four walls left me a lot of time to reflect on my life and happier days. I remembered finishing up third grade and the freedom I felt on summer vacation. In third grade I wrote and published my first short story: everything you needed to know about my cat, Max. That was the first and last book I enjoyed writing as a child; instead, crafting became my happy place. My best friend, Kristin, and I created K.A.T. crafts, short for Kristin and Tracy. While I can't remember what we made, I loved being in business. When we were not crafting, Kristin, my sister, and I rode our bikes, played soccer, and swam in our pool.

People described me as mature for my age. The two loves of my life were my dad and my ultimate love: Patrick Swayze. I met and fell in love with Patrick watching *Dirty Dancing* for the first time. I didn't realize it at the time, but my dad, Mr. Fix-It, had edited out all the "mature" scenes, leaving me with the fun dancing parts, and of course Patrick's tight tushy. When it was time for the father-daughter dance in Girl Scouts, my dad and I practiced "the lift" in our living room for over an hour. I could recite every single line from that movie and the soundtrack was constantly playing on my Girl Talk radio. Life was great.

Another thing I loved about summer was having my mom around during the day. She had the summers off as a teacher and her running joke was saying that she ran Camp Lipsky. Our house was where all the kids in the neighborhood hung out. My mom was constantly cutting up watermelon, preparing snacks, and stopping me from picking on my younger sister, Amanda.

All the time I spent watching *Dirty Dancing,* Amanda could be found watching *The Mighty Ducks.* Amanda and I couldn't be more different if we tried. I was into fashion, looking good, and being neat. All she wanted to do was play sports. Art supplies were crammed into every nook and cranny of her bedroom. Her style was distinct and very different from mine. My mom teased us, "If I could just mix the two of you together, I would have a perfectly balanced child."

Every Friday during the summer, my aunt had off from work. My mom, sister, and I often joined my aunt and cousin for fun in the sun. We kicked it off with Dunkin' Donuts on the way to the beach. This was a huge treat, evidenced by our wide, sugary smiles. Hopping back into the car, we jammed out to Big D 103 all the way to Hammonasset Beach or Rocky Neck State Park. My cousin and I sang at the top of our lungs to the Beach Boys and the Righteous Brothers. My sister, Amanda, would shake her head, looking at us like we were insane. Even at ten, I felt like I was sixteen and ready for the runway in my fashionable two-piece bathing suit. We swam, played in the sand, and laughed all day.

As I lay in the hospital bed, I realized how amazing my childhood truly was. I longed to relive the freedom and fun of my glory days with my own children, Alyssa and Matthew. My memories were bittersweet, knowing they were back home missing me and being robbed of our fun times too.

# MY STORM BUNKER

Being away from home for so long was excruciatingly hard. I missed my kids like crazy. When I looked around my room at all the pictures, my children's cute little faces and their latest schoolwork cheered me up at times. Other times it sent sharp stabs of sadness through me, making me miss my home life even more. My mother-in-law saved each and every paper from the kids' schoolwork for me, and all the nurses loved to visit me. They enjoyed checking out the Kearcher Art Museum and we'd exchange our favorite "mommy" moments: little jokes our kids said, or things they did that cracked us up.

I loved these intimate moments. For a second here and there I forgot I was stuck in the hospital, fighting for my life. For a few moments I was back to the days of exchanging casual conversation with fellow moms at the local park on a beautiful sunny day. It wasn't until the nurses left and the four sterile walls of my room stared back at me, that I was reminded: my little ones were miles away and I was stuck, confined to the hospital.

Thank goodness for FaceTime and the latest technology. I eagerly looked forward to seeing Matthew's forehead each night (he did not know how to properly hold the cell phone), and Alyssa's nonstop talking, telling me about her school day and speaking way too loud into the phone. I smile even now as I think about those calls. There were times I laughed out loud at their cute remarks and other times when I held back my tears, desperately trying to stay strong for them. They had enough to worry about already.

I was heartbroken over all the precious mommy moments I was missing. My in-laws saw Matthew's eyes light up when he saw them, his mimi and papa K, at preschool dismissal, not me. Facebook became my portal to the outside world as I spent hours scrolling and catching lopsided glimpses of people's lives. Stuck in the hospital, looking at the same four walls day after day, I walked the hallways longing to escape Cancer Land. Facebook and television only offered momentary relief.

Luckily, Matthew attended preschool. By the time I was diagnosed, he was already established in the town's preschool program with amazing teachers. The almost-daily emails from his main teacher, Mrs. Mags (how Matt referred to her), were a gift. She also sent me pictures. I treasured every update and picture, rereading the words and lingering over the snapshots of my son. They gave me a window into his life and world.

My children's elementary school staff chipped in and gave my family a gift card to a local pizza restaurant. It arrived in a beautiful gift basket. The Ellington Girl Scouts and MOMS Club held fundraisers for my family, and some moms from Ellington organized an ice cream fundraiser at Kloter Farms, a local ice cream stand. In the midst of this difficult season, I was deeply touched by how many people from Ellington, and even past friends from Middletown and former coworkers, came to support us. It felt miraculous.

My friends, family, and loved ones started a prayer community that quickly spread all over the United States. When my faith was depleted and I questioned everything, these prayers and the well wishes of complete strangers carried me. The steady stream of get-well cards, comfortable socks, coloring books, and healing prayers encouraged me and boosted my hope. Just knowing that people were praying for my family fueled my confidence and strength. Some of my former hairdressing clients even sent hand-drawn pictures. My sister created a well-wishes book to hold and display all of them. To this day, it's on my nightstand. As alone as I sometimes felt in my hospital room, the book continued to remind me just how connected and loved we are. I hope you feel it too as you read these words: You are loved. You are not alone.

My father bought my husband a book of prayer. Many times, throughout the long days, we prayed together. One of my mother's close friends sent us this prayer by Father Larry J. Hess,

> Every breath I take, every morning I wake, and every moment of every hour, I live under your power.
>
> For if you created me from nothing, you can certainly recreate me.
>
> Fill me with the healing power of your spirit...
>
> And **Father**, restore me to full health in mind, body, and spirit, so I may serve you the rest of my life.

Thankfully, our friends and neighbors were eager to help; all their kindness and effort became a welcome comfort and support to me and my family. My sister-in-law and husband constantly updated my website so others could sign up to make my family dinner and arrange playdates for my kids. It also saved me from having to update people individually, providing frequent updates on my treatment and future plans. Being a stay-at-home mom, I was the constant anchor and rock for my kids, emotionally and physically. While Tim and his parents were doing an amazing job trying to manage all my previous responsibilities, there was still a great need. My mother-in-law joked and said it took all three of them to do what I did on an average day before I became ill.

My sister, Amanda, is a social worker and she went above and beyond to ensure that my children coped as well as could be expected under our dire circumstances. She brought home children's books explaining all about mom's new hats and why I suddenly had no hair; she even bought my daughter and I matching bandannas. When I lost my hair, my daughter was the most upset. She was afraid people would make fun of me. Her caring heart was beautiful to witness, and I told her, "Let them make fun of it. It won't bother me in the least." To myself, I knew I had much more important matters to worry about (like staying alive).

# THE STORM WITHIN

was in the hospital for thirty-eight consecutive days. The nurses gave me the corner room to keep me out of high traffic areas, and all the germs that came with them. I stared out the window at the same brick wall for my entire stay. If I wanted to shake things up, I'd sit in a tiny corner nook and watch as ambulances pulled in with other patients. I'd wonder if they had leukemia too, or if they did but didn't know it yet. I daydreamed about life in pre-Cancer Land.

If I felt well enough, I walked the same hallways each day and ate from the same boring options of the "limited fully cooked" menu. I knew all the choices off the top of my head, just as I knew exactly how many steps it took to get to the end of the hallway, twenty-five. I even knew where the extra boxes of tissues were stored. The hospital was the home I never wanted that I quickly learned my way around. One night, my cousin Cheryl brought me a fresh, hot delicious pizza pie from New Haven for some variety. I can still smell the hot cheese and warm scent filling up my bland hospital room. It was the type of pizza people travel to Connecticut for. Savoring each bite, I took three before I threw it all back up. What a waste of a delicious pizza pie. But maybe it wasn't because I still remember Cheryl's kindness and the joy of those three bites.

I knew I needed to eat as much as possible so my body could heal. It was hard, but I kept taking baby bites and praying for the food to stay down this time. There were days I became ill more times than I could count. Other days I felt nauseous all day long. I did my best to keep my mind busy because it was easy for discouragement, grief, and pain to take over. I picked up my latest craft project or continued my *Blue Bloods* marathon. The less I dwelled on how miserable I felt, the better.

Each day of my recovery had a number. The first day after all the chemotherapy was done was Day 1. It wasn't until I was in the late thirties that doctors considered releasing me to go home. The days passed slowly as I prayed for my strength to return and tried to rest.

Three times a day, pill time arrived. Throughout the course of each day, forty pills were handed to me by a nurse. Some of them were extremely large. As I was finally getting the last of the pills down, the nurse would bring in the next dose. I will forever be grateful to the nurse who advised me to take them in chocolate pudding. The continuous medication cycle kept me alive. What a change from my pre-leukemia life: I didn't even take a daily multivitamin. In the blink of an eye, my life as I knew it was gone.

The chemotherapies I was on were well known for causing major tooth and gum problems in other patients who had undergone similar treatment. Nurses helped me brush my teeth gently and gargle with the most hideous mouthwash three times a day.

The smell of the mouthwash alone was enough to make me ill. Just typing this, I can feel my gag reflex kick in.

My body became so frail, my mom became my constant companion, supporting me to the bathroom and shower. One day the nurses came running because I was about to pass out. At thirty-four years old, I relied on a shower chair; I did not have the strength to stand up. It felt surreal, to think that taking a shower could leave one completely drained physically and mentally for hours. My mom bought me cute and comfy pajamas so I didn't have to wear the hospital gowns. It felt ironic putting them on because, for the first time in my life, I didn't care what I looked like.

Around Day 15, post-chemotherapy treatment, it was time for my second bone marrow biopsy. I dreaded the gross and extremely painful process. In short, the "specialist" at the hospital asked me to lay on my stomach. Next, he injected a needle of lidocaine into my lower hip to numb the area; it felt like a very bad bee sting. Then came the part that gave me nightmares, he used a "medical" corkscrew to screw into my hip bone and extract core bone marrow samples and liquid samples with a quick nauseating suck.

The horror movie sprang to life as the technician dug into my bone. I felt intense pressure wash over me, from slight pain to immense pain. It was a jumbled mess of nerve and bone pain, unlike anything I'd felt before. My prayers became desperate during the procedure, emerging from the depths of my being. The pain did not subside after either but lingered in my body as my back felt sore for days. Even now, the remnants remain, with my lower back covered in scars from each and every biopsy procedure.

Dad and his hand were with me for each biopsy. His calm voice and permission to squeeze the heck out of his hand eased those excruciating moments of suffering. Tim brought another super-power, scrolling through his phone for the latest pictures of our kids. I kept going for the two of them, blinking through the pain to bask in Matthew and Alyssa's smiles as they played with their friends, or pictures of popsicle juice dripping from their red-colored grins. I missed my two cuties so much!

My heart ached to hug them and hear their little giggles. How I longed to be in those photos with them, instead of lying on this freezing cold table, doubled over in pain, gritting my teeth to stay still. Sadly, the biopsy results showed there were still 20–25 percent leukemic blood cells in my marrow. It was to be expected at this point in treatment, even as we prayed for a miracle. We knew that the final bone marrow biopsy around Day 30 was when we were praying to see zero blast cells (leukemic).

The hospital recommended a peer mentor program, where I'd be connected with a cancer survivor, someone who really understood what it felt like to have one's world turned upside down. After all, they received a similar death sentence and yet, somehow, lived to tell their story. After a few days, I finally spoke with a mentor. I was looking forward to her words of wisdom, encouragement, and hope.

Instead of the conversation leaving me calmer and more at ease, it had an adverse reaction. The mentor connected to me was a patient over ten years ago. She only had one round of chemotherapy and didn't need to have a stem cell transplant. Unlike mine, her form of leukemia was less aggressive. She didn't have the devil strand known as inversion of chromosome 3. I left our conversation feeling deflated and hopeless. Did anyone understand?

Walking around the cancer ward day in and day out, I saw patients who looked like they were at death's doorstep. It was a whole new world. The sound of family members crying in the hallways was normal. To make matters worse, one night while I was alone in my hospital room, which didn't happen often, I decided to consult "Dr. Google" and searched the inversion of chromosome 3. There were no known survivors, not a single positive case in the entire Google world of anyone who had been diagnosed with the strand and lived. My body and spirit instantly deflated as I stared at the sterile walls of my room. An endless hurricane of fear and uncertainty threatened to swallow my hope and will to fight. I prayed every day to God for the doctors to discover more lifesaving options for me.

My lead oncologist reached out to a team of hematology doctors at Dana-Farber in Boston, MA, and Sloan Kettering in NYC, sharing my case with them. There were other great facilities nearby such as Smilow at Yale, where my cousin Cheryl worked. However, the collaborative group of doctors believed New York and Boston offered more advanced treatment options. We put our faith in the doctor's recommendation and agreed to go to either Boston or New York for treatment.

The window to decide was short, and after my family and I talked it over, we agreed that the next phase of my journey would be in Boston at Dana-Farber/Brigham and Women's (B&W). The facilities are adjacent to one another in the Brookline section of

Boston. B&W is a fully functional hospital with a focus on treating cancer patients, while Dana-Farber accepts outpatients next door.

Since I had AML leukemia with the inversion of chromosome 3, we knew that even in remission (God willing) I would need to undergo a stem cell transplant. My sister quickly initiated the process to see if she was a potential stem cell match. Every sibling has less than a 25 percent chance of being a perfect match, but they have greater odds than a stranger. Typically, the match is based on ancestry, so people who are 100 percent Irish are more likely to find a perfect match than someone like myself whose ancestors are a mix of various nationalities. My nurses didn't want to get my hopes up, sharing stories of patients with six siblings and not one of them a match. The odds were slim for my sister, but she was happy to try. Growing up my sister, Amanda, was always lucky and won practically every game we played on family game night. I resented her for winning all the time, but this time I hoped her magical luck shone through.

As I approached the end of my hospital stay, it felt like the whole world was praying for me and my family. My nurses were optimistic. I was a diligent fighter—surely the chemotherapy worked. After waiting for what felt like an eternity, the results from my Day 30 bone marrow biopsy were finally back. The nurses, my entire family, and the Ellington community hoped and prayed that every leukemia blast cell was eliminated.

The oncologist was late that day in arriving at the planned time—was this a bad sign that they were trying to figure out how to break the news? I held my breath when the doctor stepped into the room, the pit in my stomach growing even larger as he broke the news that there were still 6 percent blast cells present in my bone marrow. All the hard work and pain had not rid my body of the cancer. My family and I were crushed. The mood in the room was now reminiscent of when I was first admitted. I had prayed, we had prayed—where was my God when I needed him most? I didn't want to go home and face my six-year-old daughter and the question I knew she would ask, "Why did God make you sick, Mommy?" No mom is ever prepared to be asked this by her daughter. It broke my heart. Moms are supposed to know everything. They are supposed to fix all the ailments. It was my deepest desire, and my duty, to be there for my children, watch them grow up, and to guide and nurture them along their way through life. It wasn't fair. I wanted my old life back, to sleep beside my husband every night, tuck my kids into bed, pack their lunches and snacks, and be the hands-on mom I loved being.

# CALM BETWEEN THE STORMS

was finally discharged from Hartford Hospital and could celebrate Easter at home with my kids! My friends and family tried their best to make it a magical holiday for us. The Easter celebration was unlike those of past years where we'd all be dressed in our finest and attend Sunday Mass. Instead, this year we didn't leave our house and watched Mass from the Vatican. It was absolutely stunning. Perhaps God was trying to raise our spirits through the elaborate Easter Mass festivities. If Jesus rose from the dead, surely, I could beat AML leukemia. After taking in the celebration from our couch, I began to tire. Our neighbors kindly invited our kids to an egg hunt later in the morning, however my exhaustion caught up to me, and I curled up for a nap. I was sad to pass up the opportunity to watch the hunt but had no energy to watch the event.

Internally, big black clouds followed me wherever I went. Luckily, my children's excitement for Easter and having me home kept me going. That Easter remains vivid in my memory because I savored each and every moment as though it were my last. My children remember that holiday as well, for a different reason. Fellow teachers, who worked with my mom, chipped in so the Easter bunny could provide enormous Easter baskets for them. The kids played with all their new Easter goodies for hours and I loved lounging on the couch and watching them. My eyes and heart had missed them, and this was balm for my soul.

While I was home between treatments, my mom and dad took me to the Starling Physicians Infusion Center twice a week to receive intravenous liquids. My blood pressure was low even before leukemia, and I tried to drink plenty of fluids, but with the lingering nausea, it was extremely hard to stay well hydrated. I needed intravenous fluids to help me feel better and raise my blood pressure. The nurses and patients there were amazing. Each of them had their own health horror story. The patience, kindness, and sense of understanding they shared as a result was unlike any I had experienced before. Their tidbits of advice and life lessons are still with me. They told my mom where to buy the best wigs, and which nurses to request. My mom pulled out her notebook to take notes; their advice was that good. I hope each and every one of them is well.

One night, while I was home in between my hospital stays, Tim and I watched the movie *Stronger* (2017). It was the heroic tale of Jeff Bauman, a survivor of the Boston Marathon bombing. A scene mentioned the hospital where I would receive my next treatment and then progressed to show my future home for those forty long days of treatment. Jeff's life changed overnight without any warning. We watched him face various mental and physical challenges in scene after scene. Overwhelmed and undergoing treatments and therapy, he portrayed so many emotions throughout the movie. Many of these feelings I was intimately familiar with such as pain, anger, resentment, remorse, and fear. It was like watching my own story with different circumstances, everything I'd experienced since receiving my leukemia diagnosis. Watching the movie opened my emotional floodgates. I fell into Tim's arms, sobbing in hysterics as the credits rolled. I cried like I have never cried before. I must have used up all my allotted tears in life because after that day I no longer cried with tears, and most likely never will again. I was completely and utterly broken.

# LIFE BEFORE THE STORMS

The further forward I moved in my battle with leukemia, the more I found myself reflecting on my life. The daily struggles I faced before leukemia were stressful, but for the very first time I realized how blessed Tim and I truly were. I had so much to live for.

Growing up, I'd longed for a romantic story of meeting my Mr. Right. As crazy as it sounds for a woman in the twentieth century, my goal in life was to be a wife and mother. I loved being a hairdresser, but in my heart of hearts I was dying to be a mom. The endless dates I went on led nowhere; I just wasn't connecting with the right guy. Finally, one weekend I said, "That is it, I quit! I am staying home, taking my dog, Daisy, for a walk, watching a chick flick, and eating Ben and Jerry's all night long." Of course, that was also the night I was formally introduced to my condo neighbor Timothy.

The funny thing is that a year prior, when I moved into the condo complex, my mom noticed how Tim had left his running shoes outside to air them out. She commented on how "sneaker boy" was probably very neat and we had one thing in common: we both loved to run. Sneaker boy and I spent more and more time together, fell in love, and eventually set a date for our wedding: October 9, 2010.

Well, our daughter, Alyssa, had other plans for us. We were expecting. After calling our entire family, and the Catholic parish priest (I was beyond mortified), we reserved a new wedding date.

We married on April 10, 2010, and it was a beautiful wedding. To this day, people comment on the fantastic filet that was served. My dreams were coming true: a husband, home, and a beautiful baby girl, all in one year. Alyssa Rose was born in September after only six hours of delivery. She was our little angel with ten perfect fingers and ten perfect toes. Tim and I were proud first-time parents, cherishing all the first-time moments and memories. I loved bringing her to mommy-and-me music classes, art classes, and story time at the local library.

Three short years later, our Matthew Joseph came into the world, and once again, we were thrilled. I had the little girl I'd dreamed of, and Tim had his baby boy. We were the perfect all-American family. Life passed quickly, without any hiccups, until Matthew turned six months old. His right eye was not moving to the right like it should. The local eye doctors confirmed that he had an eye movement disorder. We were heartbroken that our beautiful baby boy looked different from the other kids. I worried about other people's reactions and comments. Would his classmates make fun of him? Would he be able to play sports, or drive a car?

As time went on, Matthew also experienced feeding issues. He never graduated to baby food with larger pieces in it, let alone "normal" food. The journey to specialists began and they kept repeating that he would eat when he was ready. Matthew also never put any toys in his mouth, which had me concerned. We worked with Birth to Three (a program run by the Connecticut Office of Early Childhood to strengthen the capacity of Connecticut's families to meet the developmental and health-related needs of their infants and toddlers who have delays or disabilities) but progress was extremely slow.

On top of these things, Matt had multiple sensory issues, delayed speech, and no little play friends. What he did have were bright blond curls and a killer smile that would melt any girl's heart. As parents, Tim and I just wanted Matthew and Alyssa to be happy and healthy. It became my mission in life to catch Matthew up to the other children his age. My new self-appointed work included a ton of reading and taking online classes.

I quit my part-time job and created my own traveling salon. I made my own hours to always be available for our kids. Between speech therapy sessions, occupational therapy sessions, and Birth to Three sessions, our days were full of appointments and challenges. Before Alyssa started Kindergarten in the Fall we decided to move to Ellington, Ct., because it was much closer to where Tim worked, saving him over two hours in daily commute time and providing him more of an opportunity to spend time with me and the kids. The town was also known for having a better school system and being a close-knit community.

We moved to Ellington in July 2015 and adjusting to our new life was extremely hard for me. Tim was gone all day at work and I didn't have any family or friends nearby. Alyssa was now in half-day afternoon kindergarten instead of a full-day preschool program. Matthew had an extremely hard time going anywhere out in public.

Simply getting him dressed every morning was a nightmare and battle. He screamed, flapped all around, and constantly tried to rip his clothes off. I tried all different fabrics and textures to see if any made him happier and calmer. At this time, three-years-old Matthew still didn't have the speech capabilities to tell me what was bothering him.

I tried to get connected and involved with the MOMS Club of Ellington. Between nap schedules and all of Matthew's therapy appointments, we struggled to attend their events. Even trying to run out for a gallon of milk at the local grocery store resulted with Matthew in a full-blown sensory overload meltdown. The sounds, all the people, and lights were just too much for him to process. Alyssa got mad at me because we never went anywhere or had any fun. It was easy to see why she felt as though our world revolved around Matthew, his therapy, and his special needs, because it did.

I joined the local YMCA, which provided me with some "mommy" time to work out and relieve some stress. Its child watch program allowed Alyssa to branch out and meet new kids and exposed Matthew to other kids and adults.

I reestablished Glitsy Girls Mobile Salon in the greater Ellington area and had a few glamour birthday parties and haircut appointments here and there. Those few successful moments as a hairdresser were in stark contrast to my feelings that I was failing as a mom. Friday nights were the highlight of our weekly chaos. I was the leader for Alyssa's Daisy troop and every week we had twelve kindergarten and first-grade girls over for our weekly meeting. The girls were so cute, little, and tired. Someone was always crying for their mom. Week after week, Tim came home to a kitchen, wife, and three-year-old son covered in markers, crayons, and snacks. He'd tease me with a twinkle in his eyes, "I think I need to go back to the office; I forgot something."

I wouldn't be diagnosed until March 2017. We had been in Ellington for just over a year and a half; I am thankful for the community we connected with, and the ways in which so many stepped up after my diagnosis. Throughout my battle, people continually commented on how strong and brave I was. My answer: "I had to be." Who else would support and guide my son? I let people know that while he may look like every other child out on the playground running around and having fun, he was unique and there was a reason for his behaviors. Matthew was a year behind his peers. Speaking only a few words, he spent hours lining up his Matchbox cars. Heaven forbid one was moved; his frustration was a force to be reckoned with. Who would lead the charge, fighting for the right support for him?

As for Alyssa, she struggled through kindergarten, so my husband and I decided to have her repeat it. Who could practice sight words with her and cheer her up after a bad day at school? I called my mom whenever I felt blue. Then there were the conversations about the birds and the bees and comforting her after a day full of girly drama. Tim has a hard time opening up emotionally, even to me. Trying to get him to express his feelings and frustrations was like pulling teeth. I knew my death would crush him. If I died, how would he have the strength to be there for our kids?

Giving up was not an option. I charged into the next storm.

*Two Daisys from my troop sending me love*

*Alyssa and Matthew at my Kloter Farm ice cream fundraiser*

*Tim and I on our wedding day*

*My parents, Alyssa and I with my sister at her wedding*

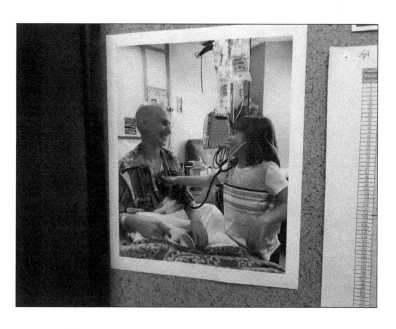

*Alyssa giving me a check up and making me laugh*

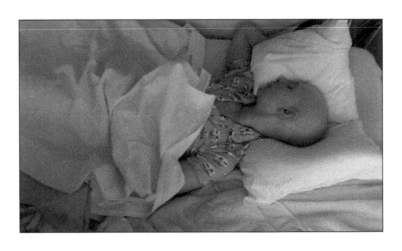

*Taking my afternoon nap*

# THE SECOND STORM

My emotions were all over the place as we drove to Dana-Farber/B&W for the second round of chemotherapy. It was extremely overwhelming because I finally felt better and I knew how hard and tiring chemotherapy was. Unlike the last time, I prepared, packed, and said my goodbyes. It didn't make it any easier to leave. On some level I thought I was in better shape for this round. Over the last few weeks, my appetite had returned and I'd put a few pounds back on. Despite this progress, I knew what I was up against and how debilitating and discouraging chemotherapy treatment was.

It was extremely hard leaving Matthew and Alyssa, knowing I would be gone for another forty days of treatment. There was no other choice if I wanted a future together as a family. Alyssa and Matthew needed me to pull through. One night I sat with Alyssa on the edge of her bed, saying, "Remember, even if I can't be home with you physically, I am always with you, in your heart." I choked back tears, wanting this to be a warm memory for her in the months, and possibly years, to come.

Brigham and Women's Hospital (B&W) was like a city within a city. It was unlike our local hospital in CT, seemingly dwarfing Hartford Hospital with its endless hallways and multiple wings. We were in awe. As we crossed through the Bridge of Hope (connecting Dana-Farber to B&W), all these beautiful birds were peering down at me; the artwork was absolutely stunning. If this vibrant mural were in a museum and not a hospital, I would have admired it for hours. At this point it felt like way too much of a tease. I wouldn't see real birds, and even these painted fake birds, for what felt like an eternity. In just a few hours, I was confined to an extremely small unit. It's probably good I didn't know beforehand, or my discouragement would have run deeper at the time of my arrival.

Walking into unit 4B, which was an airtight transplant/chemotherapy unit, I felt like I was entering a prison with friendly guards. 4B is a pod of rooms on the fourth floor of B&W. After passing the check-in area, there are approximately fifteen rooms that form a tiny tight-knit circle. My new room had a brick wall view of an adjacent building, just like I had in Hartford. My spirit dipped as I took it in—how I longed for a different view. This tiny room and teeny circular unit became my world for over a month. The air was thick with the aroma of bleach, stiff white sheets, my hideous old lady purple slippers, and wearing pajamas day after day became my life. The hairdresser in me was appalled. As a stylist, I always wore fashionable clothes, earrings, and makeup. That stylist would never recognize this Tracy. My identity and sense of self was forever impacted by that experience. Doctors and nurses constantly wore masks, and all visitors were required to sanitize their hands before entering my room—mind you this was pre-Covid.

On the plus side, the oncology nurses on unit 4B were like fairy godmothers. Their patience, diligence, and detailed care were out of this world, and the food menu had more options, including the welcome surprise of frappes (my favorite). My craft supplies were stocked and ready to keep me busy as I created barrettes and headbands. Tracy Kearcher for a Cure was up and running, ready to make a difference one creation at a time (you can find my most recent creations on Facebook @TracyKearcherforacure).

On March 5, 2017, I was as ready as I was ever going to be for my next round of salvage chemotherapy. This time it was a clinical chemotherapy trial. The knowledge of all the people who had participated in clinical trials for patients like me propelled me forward: now it was my turn to do my part. My favorite nurse, Mary Lou, with her thick Boston accent, drew a diagram on my whiteboard explaining the effect of the treatment. There was an additional "marker component" to attract the leukemic cells, making the treatment more effective. A nurse shared that some patients found it helpful to visualize the chemotherapy attacking the leukemic cells in their minds. This activity kept me busy for hours. Those nasty cancer cells were going down!

I went through all the expected stages: nausea and bowel issues. I was either going way too much or completely backed up. My diet was back to eating vanilla ice cream and red popsicles because my immune system, the lining of my esophagus, and my digestive tract had been stripped away once again. Tums were my nonstop request.

And this time the chemotherapy made my urine toxic. Nurses instructed my parents and visitors not to use my bathroom for their own personal safety. Talk about fun times.

My counting of days began, as I longed for day thirty-eight or forty, when my body would be whole again. Praying daily, "God, please let there be zero leukemic blast cells present when the treatment is done."

New hospital living routines were established. Each and every morning, I awoke for blood work. I knew what television channel to turn to for a laugh. Afterward, if I was up to it, my mom and I walked around our unit, 4B. Some days I saw some horrid sights. One day there was a man who refused to wear any clothes. My mom and I decided not to walk the rest of that day, just in case.

The sound of the snack cart was music to my ears, and I watched the minute hands until it's prompt arrival at two PM every afternoon. Even though I wasn't hungry, it meant the day was more than halfway over and I was that much closer to days thirty-eight and forty. Sometimes my daily afternoon nap went over the typical two hours, and I missed seeing my snack cart friend.

One round of pills after another, the never-ending cycle of medications kept me busy. I hated feeling the hard shapes in my mouth and constantly forcing them down with water, or chocolate pudding. My mind and body were often out of sync, and I missed having visitors. Boston was farther away from those I loved. I longed to hold my kids and smell their hair. I longed for my old life. The question lingered in my mind and in the corners of my small room, "Why, God, why?"

B&W is a nonprofit teaching hospital, which means classes of students make rounds, as well as the main doctors. Instructors talked to the classes about each patient on their rounds. My body was Exhibit A, which I didn't mind in the least. I was so desperate physically that I was willing to accept help from anyone; although, it was extremely weird being referred to as "the thirty-four-year-old patient. It felt surreal because I was always so healthy. This was the first time in thirty-four years (other than giving birth twice) I had been in a hospital, let alone lived in one.

One day, the instructor and doctor were describing in detail how I had been bleeding vaginally for weeks due to my platelet count being so low. I laughed to myself after the class left. Throughout my teenage years I was embarrassed of my period. At that moment in time, I felt like a commercial publicizing it, but the funding for the commercial was extremely low. There was no hairstylist or makeup artist. Oh yeah, I didn't have any hair. My laughter grew at the absurdity of it all.

Whenever my family and I had the strength and the words, we prayed, day after day. Growing up my dad was a Eucharistic minister and extremely religious. We often jokingly called him "The Pope." He was and still is a quiet man of convictions. During my hospital stay, he constantly kissed me on my forehead and said, "Keep fighting, my little warrior."

One day when I was feeling down and out after throwing up my recent lunch, I sensed his anger. It felt like it was radiating off him. When we were alone in the room, I asked him, "Do you want to talk?"

He poured out his frustration and shook with emotion: "How could God do this to you? You're my little girl, and we've always been faithful and followed his teachings. I just don't understand..."

His voice trailed off and it broke my heart. This was the man who was my rock, with unshakeable faith and wisdom. I felt my own world tilt with his words. How could the man who provided me with so much spiritual insight, fueling my faith, now question his own? It scared me. As I struggled with how to respond, I landed on one of my dad's famous lines. He said it throughout my childhood and into adulthood, "Life happens while you are busy making plans."

And I followed it with a heartfelt plea, "Dad, God's got to have a master plan. He must! We can't give up." My words hung in the air of my small room and my dad slowly nodded, sighed, and gazed into my eyes for a long time.

A single blood transfusion is daunting and scary to most, and throughout my treatment I received at least thirty of them, along with multiple platelet transfusions because my platelet levels were dangerously low. Bloody noses were my constant companions, as well as having the never-ending menses.

Right now, as I type this, and later, so everyone reading this hears it too, I want to say: Thank you to everyone who donates to the American Red Cross. I know, personally, for a fact, blood donations save lives. Blood donors saved mine. Each transfusion took close to two hours from start to finish. Despite how frequently I required them, each one was a bizarre experience. Someone else's blood pumped into my body.

Science has come so far, it is incredible. The blood service can now match HLA (human leukocyte antigen) platelets when needed, as in my case. After a few platelet transfusions, my levels did not rise, so doctors knew I needed HLA-matched platelets. In short, your body will recognize the foreign HLA and make antigens to destroy the cells, which is why my platelet levels did not rise. So, my "high-maintenance body" required HLA-matched platelets.

One day, about halfway through my stay, my husband and daughter surprised me with a visit during the week. Tim usually stayed with me over the weekend, but this day he showed up unannounced. Upon seeing Alyssa enter the room, I screamed, "POOK, POOK," and jumped on my bed with excitement. It was so loud that two different nurses came running into my room, "What's wrong? What's a Pook?"

I laughed, almost hysterical at this point, and breathlessly replied, "It's my daughter's nickname, ever since she was a baby." Incredibly excited to see her, I couldn't stop smiling. Tim took her out of school early to surprise me and it remains one of the best surprises of my entire life.

The nurses gave Alyssa window markers to draw me a picture. The brick view faded as she drew all over those large windows. She chatted away, filling me in on what she was learning at school and her daily life at home. We watched a cartoon movie and cuddled close together in my hospital bed. What an amazing gift, to see her in person. Her presence motivated me over the next few days; I wanted to kick leukemia's a**.

One day, upon waking up from a two-hour nap, I found myself alone. My parents were not back from their afternoon walk. I decided to check my email and noticed an email from Stacey Chuma, Dr. Antin's lead nurse. I could not believe what I was reading—my sister was a perfect stem cell match! I quickly called Amanda with the fantastic news. Tears welled up in our eyes as our voices choked back emotion. The sister I picked on and teased growing up now had the chance to save my life. It was our family's MIRACLE!

My friends, family, and I were ecstatic. A little party erupted in my room that afternoon as a wave of optimism finally appeared in the midst of my storms! It was going to be okay after all. This nightmare had a happy ending. It wouldn't take months searching for a donor or trying to make due with one that was a stretch. My sister, the one constantly by my side during treatment, was going to save my life! Now I just had to get into remission so Amanda and I could undergo the stem cell transplant.

After being in my tiny room, staring at the same four walls for over a month, it was time for another bone marrow biopsy. Had this second round of chemotherapy been successful? I looked and felt much better. Some of my energy was back and I ate more, without throwing it all up. I had, once again, been to hell and back physically and mentally. My body had responded as well as could have been expected during the clinical trial. Everyone thought the news would be positive. People were sharing their prayers and well wishes to my family and me through my website. Even my nurses were hopeful.

When my lead hematology doctor came into the room with my results, my parents and sister were present. We held our breath for the highly anticipated results from my biopsy. Instantly, the look in the doctor's eyes revealed the news was not what we were all hoping for. We were wrong. I was not in remission; the blood work tricked us. The bone marrow biopsy showed that leukemic blast cells were still present.

I could not breathe.

There was no way I could survive another round of chemotherapy. This was it, the final verdict: I was going to die. The thought of not seeing Alyssa on her wedding day, or Matthew driving a real tractor...My emotions spun into a whirlwind. Wasn't I a good person? What had I done wrong? Was my previous happiness stolen, or perhaps my good luck had simply run out? How could I tell, let alone face, my kids, who were so innocent? I couldn't face them or put on a strong front for them. I was going to die. At the age of thirty-five, my life was going to end.

My sister tried to calm me down, talking me through my panic attack. Her voice felt far away, floating somewhere outside my ragged breathing. My mom and dad escaped into the hallway, consumed with their own mental breakdowns. Tim was beyond devastated too. We had done everything right. We'd listened to all the doctors' and nurses' advice and recommendations. How could this be happening? Why?

I could not catch my breath. The feeling of those moments is vivid, even now. No matter how big a breath I took, it was not enough... I had done everything the nurses told me to, I was sick for months, threw up more times than a person could count, and had finally gotten my energy back. I was feeling great; my numbers and labs were looking awesome. My family, the nurses, and I were sure the clinical trial had worked. In my head, I had been prepared to go home and catch up with my kids before the stem cell transplant, and after that final recovery, I would resume my "old" life again.

The nurses put me on oxygen to ease my anxiety attack. Their kind eyes and soft words were trying to calm my inner storm. I couldn't get enough air. There were just a few hours before I was going to be discharged. Dr. Antin, the transplant specialist at Dana-Farber, was coming to talk to my family and me about the remaining options.

We already knew my case was far from ideal. If I was in remission, my chances of the leukemia coming back post-transplant greatly decreased. Antin explained that I needed to undergo the transplant; it was the only option I had left. We would make it work. There was no other way.

# PREPARING FOR THE EYE
# OF THE STORM

Tim worked with the insurance liaison to rush the approval for my transplant. The liaison program was an initiative through our health insurance carrier to place caretakers in touch with someone they could contact at all times. The sooner the transplant, the less time the leukemic cells had to take back my bone marrow. Getting approval for a stem cell transplant is not as simple as receiving the okay for a yearly physical. There's a substantial approval process that has to take place before the hospital will proceed with the stem cell transplant. The facility needs assurance that they will be compensated for my stay and the insurance carrier working on the behalf of the employer needs to vet documentation of my case to ensure the transplant is necessary. We're extremely fortunate that Tim's employer, the Antonacci family, has made it a priority that employees and their families are given the option for a health insurance plan that provides coverage in times like this. In fact, throughout my ordeal, the owners would periodically check in with Tim to see what the latest was on my condition and prognosis. Not to mention, they would always make sure that we weren't running into any delays in getting approval for my many treatments.

I remember the stacks of paper Dr. Antin brought to my bedside for me to sign before they could begin the transplant approval process. Many of the disclaimers warned of the possible side effects, impact, and long-term effects this decision could have on my life, but my options were limited to two at this point. As he read through form after form, I began to lose focus on what each form was for, as they began to blur together. Dr. Antin and his team's commitment were my second miracle. The storms were not over yet.

The next two weeks were filled with day-long appointments at Dana-Farber with pretests and preparing for the transplant. It felt as though every inch and part of me was tested: my lungs, heart, and other body parts, everything that had been stressed with the two previous rounds of chemotherapy. All of me still needed to undergo the most taxing storm, my transplant.

When we went to Dana-Farber for the pretransplant testing, my dad was my cheerleader for the day and my sister, Amanda, was also there for her pretesting to be my donor. She had her husband, John, cheering her on. They married the previous September and I felt awful dragging them into my war. By the end of each day, we were exhausted. The pretesting was rough, every inch of our bodies poked and prodded. One speck of humor was my brother-in-law John falling asleep on a teeny tiny couch in one of the waiting rooms. My sister was right, he could sleep anywhere.

During a family meeting, we discussed what my pretransplant chemotherapy looked like, and the details of the transplant for both

Amanda and me. This was the strongest chemotherapy treatment of them all.

The storm clouds over my head grew bigger and bigger as the meeting progressed. I felt like I was drowning in an endless abyss of steps and precautions I had to take. My life depended on it, and yet it would never look the same. My house was to be cleaned from top to bottom by a team of neighbors and friends and its walls were going to be the boundary of the only place I could enter and stay, besides Dana-Farber. Unable to leave, I was limited in my activities. Dishwashing, slicing food to cook, and gardening were off the table. If either of our children were to become ill, I'd be shipped away to stay with my parents. Activities I took for granted were now part of the nonnegotiable exclusions I was to avoid: no more conferences or open houses at my children's school, no more Sunday church, or restaurants. Even my basement was off-limits and my passion, cutting hair, was included in the things I could no longer do.

The long list also included limitations on who could come into my home. The only visitors allowed needed to be part of my care team and fully vaccinated. Although I was encouraged to spend as much time as possible outside, sun exposure was a risk to be cautious of because it could exacerbate graft-versus-host symptoms. If I was out taking a walk and someone was cutting the grass, I had to turn around and walk the other way. There would be no fresh foods for the first one hundred days post-transplant. The team continued on and on with the list of what I couldn't do. I drifted into desperate prayers that the transplant would be successful. Yes, I was willing to do whatever was necessary.

The only place I could go, besides my home, was Dana-Farber for my follow-up appointments. Suited up in a T25 mask and gloves, I brought my own prepared food. The world became a dangerous place for me. I felt like I was struggling to swim in all the medical terminology. The massive book I was given, with all the precautions, possible side effects, do's and don'ts, would take an intelligent, healthy individual months to read and digest. I felt as though I had been convicted of a crime in a foreign land. The words swirling around me didn't make sense and I struggled to process everything happening to me. If only God would tell me the crime I had committed, the reason for my sentence to life in prison. There were no lawyers or witnesses testifying on my behalf and time was running out.

Meanwhile, a second Hickman Port was inserted to prepare for my transplant. A Hickman port is a narrow tube inserted into a vein slightly above the collarbone, near the base of one's neck. Then it is tunneled under the skin and comes out just above one's chest. Two parallel ports were inserted in me. The scars remind me of how awful it was. Maintaining and keeping the Hickman port clean was vital to avoid a life-threatening infection, and my stay at the hospital continued. Nurses checked me daily for blood clots and flushed the lines. The taste of saline lingered in my mouth afterward. Next, they changed the cap on the end of the catheter and my dressing. Yuck, yuck, yuck! I looked away and imagined myself elsewhere, anywhere. Just the idea of what they were doing, let alone that they were doing it to me, made me queasy.

Whenever I took a shower, the nurses covered up the port area and used bandages and medical tape to cover my entire Hickman line. After the shower, the nurses gently ripped the bandages off, flushed my lines, and changed my dressing. The girl who hated needles and couldn't stand the sight of blood now lived with tubes coming out of her chest. I felt like a character from an alien movie.

When the nurses prepared me for the surgery to install the port, I told them they were making a mistake. If I was going to have any surgery done on my chest, I wanted it to be for bigger boobs, not a port. They laughed and said I had a great sense of humor! The funny thing is, I really would have loved bigger boobs while I was there!

# FLASHBACK

Throughout my life I heard the phrase, "God only gives you what you can handle." As a sophomore in high school, I decided to join the cross-country team. To prepare over the summer, I went for short runs and watched what I ate. What started off as a healthy endeavor quickly became an obsession. Little by little I increased my running distance and restricted more and more of what I ate. People noticed how I thinned out and complimented me on how I looked.

As a middle schooler I loved the freedom of coming home to an empty house and eating any afternoon snack I desired. To this day, my mom and dad tease me about picking out all the cherries and the chocolate chunks in a Cherry Garcia ice cream.

It took many hours of therapy to unpack how I thrived on the sense of control I felt with my "healthy diet." I was scared of becoming an adult, going off to college, and soaring on my own. What I didn't know at the time was how powerful our minds can be. My eating disorder quickly took control of me, dominating my every thought.

I battled with anorexia for many years. As I was trying to eat more after therapy, my disorder changed from anorexia to bulimia. It was a very lonely period in my life. Since food was my number-one obsession, I put God and my family and friends on the back burner. I weighed myself daily. Family dinnertime and parties were emotional nightmares, full of frustration, anger, and remorse.

It is a part of my past I am not proud of, even though overcoming the eating disorders made me mentally and physically stronger. As an adult and mother of two children, I learned the gift our bodies truly are. For the last few years before my diagnosis, my focus changed from trying to be the thinnest in the room to fueling my body for energy, health, and endurance. During the chemotherapy treatments, as I lost weight and had trouble eating and keeping food down, my mom and I reflected on the years I struggled with the disorders and my body image. For the second time in my life, I was skin and bones, but this time it wasn't due to my eating disorders. This time it was leukemia's fault.

# RESCUE FROM THE STORM?

On June 13, 2017, the day before my thirty-fifth birthday, my parents and I drove to Boston. It was time to harvest my leukemic stem cells to make a leukemia vaccine for another clinical trial I participated in. The transplant had been approved by our insurance provider and necessary preparations were now in place. As my dad drove I rested in the back seat, staring out the window at the passing scenery, I thought about Matthew. It felt like he had just started preschool, then I was diagnosed, and now he was already finished for the year. My heart ached for all the precious moments I had lost with him.

Matthew and I were inseparable when he was a baby and toddler. I watched him walk his little blue car up and down our driveway for hours. When we were living in Middletown, the two of us walked down to the main road to sit on the sidewalk and watch the cars go by. His favorite thing in the entire world was "rucks" (trucks) and I can still hear his little voice shouting, "Rucks, Mom! Rucks!" I missed being the one to see his eyes light up every time he saw one.

Summer vacation was beginning at the end of the week, and I would miss it all. There would be no building sandcastles or laughing in the waves at the beach, no embarking on a family vacation, bike rides, or outings to the local ice cream parlor. My heart ached and I held back tears. Would the next treatment and transplant even work? Summer is my favorite season of the year, and I was to be imprisoned inside the walls of 4B for what seemed to be an eternity. It was too much to take in, an overwhelming nightmare. Was this really my life? I constantly battled to bring my focus back to my main goal: living and returning to my family, kids, and home. Desperation clawed at my chest. I wanted so much to be healthy once again.

The bone marrow biopsy and having my core sample extracted for the vaccine was a blur. Driving home with my parents, I kept the ice pack on my back for the entire two-hour ride. That night, as I ate dinner with my family and spent quality time with my kids before my readmittance into the hospital in two days, I tried to soak up every moment with all my senses—if only I could bottle up all their giggles, adorable facial expressions, and love and bring them with me.

The next day, while my kids were at school, the phone rang. The urgency in the voice of the lead nurse told me it was serious. There were not enough leukemic cells in my core sample to make a vaccine. I needed to leave immediately for my long "transplant" hospital stay, as the doctors needed another core sample to complement the first one.

I frantically called Tim, quickly updating him before rushing to gather my belongings: the mandatory brand-new pillow, new slippers, shower shoes, and button-up pajamas. I left notes and pictures for my kids, kissing the papers before I laid them down on their beds, praying they would know how much I loved them. Then my parents and I were on our way. The K-Love radio station played on the car radio and reminded me to *Just Breathe*. "*God will carry you through the storm*" (Isaiah 43:2).

The conditioning chemotherapy pretransplant was the strongest yet. It didn't take long to feel the effect. The very first day, I was violently ill. I knew the chemotherapy was making room in my bone marrow for Amanda's healthy stem cells, but the knowledge didn't stop the impact.

Amanda took medication prior to the harvesting of her life-saving stem cells for my transplant. She underwent apheresis, a process that extracted the stem cells from her blood plasma. It took two days for her to produce enough stem cells for my transplant, which is both uncomfortable and very common.

I received dose one on the twenty-first of June and the final stem cells were injected into my spine on the twenty-second. Would it work?

I claimed June 22nd as my new "rebirth" date, and it is forever etched in my memory and story. My entire family prayed harder than ever; we knew what it was like to have our hope crushed and this just had to work. A minister even blessed my sister's stem cells before the transplant.

# MY STEM CELL TRANSPLANT PRAYER

Most merciful God, Creator, and Sustainer,

You are the fountain and source of all. We come before you humbled by your great gift of life. In your infinite love, you composed us of tiny cells and gave them the power to sustain, heal, and renew. For giving scientists, physicians, and nurses the knowledge to transplant healthy cells for others' well-being, we give you thanks. For providing Tracy's sister, Amanda, to be her stem cell donor, we give you thanks. For the loving support of family, parents, Marilyn and Joseph, her husband, Tim, and children, Alyssa and Matthew, we give you thanks. For having brought us to this special day, we give you thanks.

You are the Great Healer and Physician, and we acknowledge that all healing comes from you.

Bless these stem cells; bring your healing and new life to Tracy today. May Tracy trust you not only in the power you have given these stem cells to heal, but also in your invitation to spiritual rebirth. Give Tracy patience and hope as we wait for the restoration of her body, mind, and spirit. Please send your Spirit upon these cells, blessing them with your love and healing power so that they bring about full and complete restoration to Tracy's body.

In the name of the Father, Son, and Holy Spirit, we pray. AMEN

# RESCUE?

I t was finally time to receive my life-saving treatment. We prayed and hoped that despite not being in remission, the transplant succeeded. The process of the actual transplant was similar to a blood transfusion. The difference was that instead of blood, healthy stem cells were pumped into my body. Drifting off to sleep that night, I felt a constant tingling along my spinal cord. It reminded me of the soda fizz that races to reach the top of the cup after being poured. "I receive your healing. Please heal me." With each tingling sensation I was praying and crossing all my fingers and toes for the transplant to work.

The true work was after my stem cell transplant. My body began the process of rebuilding itself, cell by cell. For the third time my intestinal lining was stripped away. The neutropenic fevers were back, and I was in a different room from my previous visit. A prior patient purchased a large-screen television and donated it to the transplant unit. Buckets of gratitude still well up in me, wanting to thank that random patient for their generosity. My parents came each and every day to stay with me. Their presence broke up the long monotonous days as they arrived shortly after I woke up and stayed until visiting hours were over.

There was a program for family members called Hospitality Homes. People loaned out a part of their homes to family members of patients seeking treatment at B&W. These complete strangers saved my family from financial hardship. At the time, to stay in a hotel in Downtown Boston was expensive and multiple stays could easily have pushed us to financial hardship and even ruin. My family and I are forever grateful for their extreme kindness.

Meanwhile, my mom and I were back to walking as many laps around the tiny unit as I could physically manage. Movement is not only a sign of life, but it was critically important to healing and strengthening my body. I felt like the tigers and lions we saw at the zoo, pacing back and forth, back and forth. It was like being in prison, except that if I broke out, I would not survive.

Unfortunately, I developed pneumonia and fluid buildup in my lungs. When I swallowed liquids, they went down the wrong pipe. A feeding tube was the solution and I absolutely hated this. Although I was still ravenous at times, I could not eat solids. The side effect of the intravenous food was a dangerous spike in my blood sugar, so insulin shots were added to my daily routine.

As my body took the hits and all the things I dreaded became my reality, my pity party bells rang. How much can I take? I hated this life. I didn't do anything wrong. Why was this happening to me? The darkness of my thoughts must have been reflected on my face because my parents, and Tim when he visited, looked frightened for me. Would I make it?

Finally, after about two weeks of prayers and antibiotics, I began to see and feel progress. My annoying feeding tube was removed; although, the nurses continued to monitor how much I ate and drank. There were scans to ensure the food and liquids were being digested correctly. On one occasion I warned the technician administering the test that I felt extremely nauseous.

She said, "You'll be just fine, go ahead and drink this."

It was a thick, gooey, shake-like mixture. So I did. It quickly came back up all over her. To this day, every time I see a vanilla milkshake, I think of that poor technician.

My strength returned slowly, and my mom and I added laps to our daily trek around unit 4B. If one day I walked twelve laps, the following day I came up with a higher goal and would walk around the loop fourteen times. These seemingly small milestones provided me with motivation; I was doing it! Hope emerged and I drank as many protein smoothies as I could. Little by little my energy increased, and things were looking up. Eagerly, I looked forward to returning home, where my kids, husband, and own bed waited for me. What a wondrous thing it would be to sleep through the night without vital checks, beeping, and constantly being poked and prodded.

# MY REBIRTH

Only time would tell if the transplant was successful. At this time there were no leukemic blast cells present in my routine blood work which was a very good sign. I wouldn't have a bone marrow biopsy for quite some time. Black clouds were still above in the distance my family and I were told full remission status was three years post stem cell transplant.

A new Tracy was emerging on many different fronts. From my sister's cells replacing my once deadly blood cells to learning what it feels like to have to slow down and just live in the moment. I was beginning my new life as a survivor. Small victories like keeping my drinking water down kept me motivated and encouraged for the possibility of life ahead.

I was eager to be released from the hospital. As soon as the nurses mentioned that I needed to keep fluids down to leave, I downed four bottles of Aquafina water within three hours. This was more than I had consumed in days. Home and my children were pulling at my heart. It was too long and hard of a journey to waste any more time in Hartford Hospital for.....

Then came the thick stack of discharge paperwork from Brigham and Women's; it felt like a novel. Simply skimming the to-do and not-to-do lists was exhausting. Even my mom looked like she was about to be ill. I reminded her of the mantra she repeated to me throughout my childhood and battle, "Just take it one step at a time." So that is exactly what we did.

It felt surreal to be driving home from the hospital, hopefully leukemia free.. My mom, dad, and I were quietly reflective as the K-Love radio station played on the radio. This was a monumental step and I felt like a tangled mess of emotions, both excited and nervous. Tim, along with a group of friends and relatives, had spent the prior day cleaning and scrubbing our house to ensure it was spotless and in line with the post-transplant protocols. We were all filled with questions and overflowing gratitude as we stepped into this new chapter in our journey.

Cars whipped by on the highway and the hairdresser's story from my very first hospital stay came to mind. As she shaved my hair, she said, "You're going to make it to the other side! Heck, I fought leukemia and won." Later in our conversation, she shared that a few months after her remission, her mom passed away from a heart attack.

Questions from the recent storms and battles still swirled in my mind and I desperately prayed, "God, please keep my mom healthy for an EXCEPTIONALLY long time!" Thankfully, at the time of writing this, he has continued to answer this prayer.

The car pulled into our driveway, and as I stepped into my house with my parents' help, I basked in the wonder and beauty of coming home. My mom heated up some soup for me to take with my afternoon pills. Two spoonfuls of the chicken noodle soup and I vomited once again, this time into the kitchen garbage. Welcome home, Tracy!

# REBUILDING FROM THE RUBBLE

My mom took early retirement from teaching to become my main caregiver and cheerleader. She gave up a part of herself that she loved for me, without even a moment's hesitation. The life she loved came to a stop for two full years, to save mine. Her needs moved to the backburner because my personal care was all-consuming.

The local pharmacist knew my mom by first name. From massaging my aching feet, to constantly keeping my bathroom clean to adhere to the post-transplant protocols, she was there. Day after day, she cared for my children so I could rest. She reminded Alyssa and Matthew, "Who is number one right now?" My kids replied, "Mommy." My mom knew from years of experience that if I didn't take care of myself and rest when I needed to, I would never be able to take over the reins of mommy hood.

A week after getting discharged from the hospital, I attended my sister-in-law Hilary's wedding reception outside. We decided it was best that I be a guest instead of a bridesmaid as planned. The wig I wore was so itchy, I only wore it twice after that. It was so good to be out and about in the land of the living. Alyssa was a flower girl for the third time in her life and looked like a little princess. Tim and my father kept giving me stares, reminding me to stay away from everyone.

After a while, I felt the tiredness settling over me. Matthew and I returned to my parents' house. The two of us curled up on the couch and watched a movie. As I snuggled my young son, I felt profound contentment and hope that my isolation would eventually lift completely. Some of my parents' parent's friends also cleaned their houses from top to bottom, following post-transplant protocol, so I could escape the party and rest there if I needed to. This was just one instance of the generous kindness and love we experienced throughout the entire nightmare. It was out of this world, and I am forever grateful!

My body was still not my own as my team of doctors decided it was best to keep one Hickman port in my chest until more time had passed. Two days a week a visiting nurse came to check my vital signs, see how I was eating and drinking, and tend to my port. The other days it was my responsibility to flush out the port myself. My stomach turned every time, it made me so queasy, but I knew it could get infected if it was not well maintained, and that was the last thing I needed.

It was hard accepting that my body would take time to heal. I was still so weak that a rest was required when I walked from my bedroom to the kitchen even though they were on the same floor. I stood still between the rooms, sometimes leaning on a piece of furniture, trying to catch my breath before continuing on the rest of the way.

The hospital mantra of never going to the bathroom alone continued at home. My mom or husband stayed with me to make sure I didn't pass out. The same woman who delivered two children naturally, ran a half marathon, and worked out five times a week with P90X was too weak to take a shower by herself.

My stomach shrank during the chemotherapy treatments, so I tried to eat many mini meals throughout the day, and even in the middle of the night sometimes. I felt like a mouse sneaking into the kitchen for a midnight snack. I craved salty snacks. Popcorners and chips were now my best friends.

My body and my home life were in a state of utter chaos. While I was away, our children were the center of attention and got away with a lot. Everyone was afraid for my life so they were spoiled with extra attention, gifts, and playdates. All those things faded away when I went into remission and returned home. It was people's way of giving us time to reconnect and heal as a family, but now Tim and I needed the kids to help around the house.

A few weeks after I came home, I asked my daughter to clean up her toys around the house. Irritated, she said, "I liked it better when you were in the hospital!"

It broke my heart. All my time and energy was put into fighting leukemia, and even now, as I healed, this was for her and our family. Tim and my mom quickly took her aside to talk. I understood what Alyssa was feeling. When I was sick, there was a seemingly never-ending stream of cards, gifts, and food. Now that I was home, all the pomp and circumstance was over. She missed her spotlight and the "extra attention."

Now all she had was a weak mother and a return of the daily chores she hadn't done in over a year. As for my son, Matthew, he felt betrayed by my leaving. How could a three-year-old understand why his mother suddenly left? Even now, as a five-year-old, he went to every other available adult when he needed something or had a boo-boo. It was like I didn't even exist. It took him, my Cubby Bear, a long time to come back around.

Since there was no way we could go on a family vacation to the shore like we have always done, we decided for a local day trip to the beach. My parents, Amanda, and John joined us on our adventure. My strict instructions from Dr. Antin included not to use public restrooms and to pack my own food and drinks. I was supposed to go number two before heading off to the beach with my entourage, as if that's something that can be scheduled, and was instructed to stay under the beach umbrella with a large hat and lathered in sunscreen. My parents and I laughed all the way home over those instructions. With all the different medications I was on, my digestive system was a complete mess. I had absolutely no control over my bowels.

At the beach I felt like a fragile porcelain doll in a glass display looking out at the living. It felt strange but good to be out and about, alive, and with my family. On a side note, the stars aligned and I followed all the doctor's orders. We had a fun time. It was so refreshing to be together, experiencing an adventure as a family again.

That summer, we decided it would be best for the kids to attend day camps so all the adults could stay focused on me regaining my strength. My parents and in-laws took turns cleaning our house, keeping us stocked with groceries, and driving the kids back and forth to all their activities and camps.

While those around me were constantly moving, it felt like I was traveling in slow-motion compared to the rest of the world. Tired and nauseous, I fought exhaustion and still needed to nap every day. One day I took a bath, trying to relax. Suddenly, strips of my dead and darkened, chemo-fried skin came off in the tub. I was literally molting.

Over the long months of healing and resting, I often looked down to see skin, bones, and bruises. I gave myself pep talks because looking in the mirror was so dismal and discouraging. My days included a never-ending lineup of post-transplant medications: antibiotics, vitamin supplements, and immune-suppressants, I was taking them all. There were over twenty pills to take each day. My pill tray held and kept the endless assortment organized. The rhythm of each day was centered around taking my medicine: morning, midday, and at bedtime. It was a constant struggle to get all the pills down, and then keep them down.

I was thankful for the late-summer weather because I was able to see friends and family, as long as we kept some distance between us and met outside. My spirits soared as I saw familiar faces and finally caught up with the people I loved. Because it was safer for me to be outside than inside post-transplant, my family took a few short local trips, like peach picking, mini golfing, and ice cream. Stepping out of the house, I breathed a little deeper and my muscles relaxed. My hopes for a return to normalcy, or at least some version of it, were strengthened. The fresh air and time with my family restored some of what my months inside the hospital walls had stolen.

Beyond thrilled to be living again, I missed the old Tracy. The woman who didn't have to sit down all the time, who was capable of running alongside and keeping up with her kids. She didn't have to plan around all her shortcomings. Would I ever feel like my old self? Would this nightmare of never-ending pills and restrictions ever end?

My care team at the hospital's first goal was for me to make it one hundred days post-transplant and still be in remission. My thoughts and prayers constantly returned to this: please let me stay in remission. The big black cloud of not knowing hovered on the horizon as I struggled to take baby steps forward and mentally push the storm clouds away. At night, I often lay awake, my heart pounding in my chest, as though I had just sprinted across a room. The lingering doubt and anxiety were the biggest reminders of the trauma my heart and body endured.

It was difficult rebuilding my life and body at the same time. My mom reminded me to keep my goals small. First, I walked from my bedroom to the kitchen. As fortune would have it, when we moved, we left a two-story house and moved into a one-story contemporary. Having all rooms on one floor helped my rehabilitation, something we never considered when moving. Had we still been living in a two-story house the stairs would have posed a challenge. Once I achieved the goal of walking from bedroom to kitchen, I set a goal of walking to the end of my driveway. That took me a week to conquer. Finally, I slowly increased my walking distance. "Never go too far on your own, Tracy," Mom said. I listened, scared of what might happen if I pushed myself too far.

When summer came to an end and the kids returned to school, I longed to attend the school's open houses, meet their teachers, and see what they were working on. I wondered if the teachers thought I didn't care. If only they knew how hard I fought to live, for my family. Tracy before Cancer Land volunteered every week, reading with a loud and animated voice to my daughter's kindergarten class. Alyssa loved showing me off to her friends. Knowing I did not have the strength or health to read to my son's kindergarten class and give him those same precious memories broke my heart. As much as I celebrated being alive, there were also layers of grief and loss to process and work through.

Dana-Farber was still my home away from home as my parents and I drove into Boston for my follow-up appointments. We spent hours in the car listening to the K-Love station and in floor eight's waiting rooms. I did my best to stay upbeat and positive, even though frustration reared its head over each delay. It felt like my life was on permanent hold.

Sitting in the waiting room, I knew there were other patients receiving heartbreaking news at that very moment. I looked out at my fellow cancer warriors, people from all different backgrounds. There were those who looked like they should have been admitted weeks ago to a hospital and others sat in a daze, probably brand-new to this foreign Cancer Land. Because of Dana-Farber's renowned cancer specialists, people traveled from all over the world to seek treatment. We were lucky, it was only two hours to Boston, and then two hours back home, even if it was much longer when the traffic was bad. During the long hours in the waiting room, we sometimes struck up conversations with fellow patients and their caregivers. Other times we were too tired and defeated; we sat there zoning out, hour after hour.

Alyssa's birthday was early September and we celebrated with a Trolls-themed birthday party outside. It was so fun to see Alyssa and her friends in action: playing games, eating pizza, and blowing out her candles. I cherished each and every moment of that loud and crazy kids' party. Then in November, Matthew was turning four, and for the first time, he wanted a birthday party too. I was so excited for him. For the first time, he finally had a group of his own friends. Preschool opened his world to new possibilities. Since the party was indoors, I could not attend. I eagerly waited for Tim and my sister-in-law to get back. They had strict instructions to take pictures of everything!

The same day, my mom and sister participated in a craft fair with a booth, Kearcher Creations for a Cure, at the Ellington Middle School. They met the mother of another stem cell transplant survivor who was also a former patient of Dr. Antin. They all agreed that he was a remarkable doctor. I will forever be thankful to him and his team for saving my life.

While everyone was out and about in the land of the living, I did my best to stay busy by baking all afternoon. I was incredibly sad to have missed Matthew's very first kids' birthday party, but I told myself there would be next year. I had survived!

# NEW CREATIONS

Sugar cookies always sparked my curiosity. I loved the vibrant colors and the perfect shine professionals achieved in the icing. They were a staple at birthday parties and bakeries. What more could you ask for in a cookie? They were creative and fun.

My mother and I baked together when I was a child, but these were well out of our comfort zone. When I decided to give them a try, it took the internet and Craftsy classes for me to bake and decorate sugar cookies from scratch in the comfort and safety of my home. I laughed over the ones I got wrong, enjoying the process and the delicious results. With each class my world and love of cookie decorating grew. I learned how to make royal icing and color it and to work with fondant and various fondant molds. Soon I was decorating cookies for every happy event and holiday. The hours spent learning about my new passion and lost in the creative flow took my mind off all my aches, worries, and pains. Being creative kept me motivated and excited for the next day. Baking was my therapy. It kept the storm clouds away, and I agree with the saying, "Good things come to those who bake."

After reaching a hundred days post-transplant, my care team's next goal was for me to reach the six-month mark still in remission. Occasionally I felt a flicker of the old Tracy, a moment here and there. Unfortunately, the chronic graft-versus-host battle was ramping up in my eyes, sinuses, and skin.

After a person has a stem cell transplant, getting a disease called graft-versus-host is highly likely. There are two forms: acute and chronic. I was lucky not to experience any major acute symptoms, but I do have chronic graft-versus-host. In my case, my sister's immune system recognized my body as foreign and was attempting to "reject" it. This was not a surprise. I was warned from my earliest conversations with Dr. Antin pretransplant how the disease could affect organs, although the severity varied between patients. Blessed to only have it affect my eyes, sinuses, skin, mouth, and joints, doctors do not consider my case severe, which is wonderful. The result is that I cannot cry tears. In one year, I counted exactly three tear droplets, even though I was sad from time to time. I must flush my sinuses daily with a saline nasal rinse. Dry mouth and frequent mouth sores are another result of the disease. My journey through Cancer Land transformed me into one high-maintenance mom.

Thankfully, there are specialists who know all about graft-versus-host and the various side effects. There were days when my eyes were constantly red and irritated. It felt like a chemical burn, from the moment I opened them in the morning until I tossed and turned in bed, trying to fall asleep. One of the ocular specialists in Boston put me on a regime of eye drops, hot compresses, and Refresh drops (preservative-free). I felt like a slave to my eyes, unable to do anything or even rest because they were painful and irritated.

One day my eyes were especially bad, and the treatment options did nothing to help. Standing in my kitchen with the cookie fan on my face, trying to cool my eyes off, I waited for the eye specialists in Boston to take my call. Both of my eyes were bright red and irritated. I wanted to scream from the pain, they hurt so bad! Thank goodness my mom quickly distracted my kids and took them out for an ice cream. I hated it when they witnessed my suffering, even though we tried to talk openly about my health with them. Finally, an answer, the specialists said to use the Refresh eye drops, wait a few minutes, and then insert the medication. There was a slight improvement, but my eyes were a constant source of irritation, physically and mentally.

As time passed, I learned a few more tricks to alleviate my chronic dry eye symptoms. Active prescription sunglasses limited the air flow near my eyes. I avoid air conditioner vents, fans, and bonfires. We also set up a whole-house humidifier, which helps greatly during the winters when the heat is on.

My immune system was still extremely weak and I constantly caught the colds the kids brought home from school. When the colds turned into upper respiratory infections, my progress reversed. Doctors compared my immune system to that of a newborn baby.

When my family and I walked around Dana-Farber, we saw so many children undergoing treatments. We decided to create a Christmas toy drive for the Boston Children's Hospital. We opened it up to the Ellington Girl Scouts and posted it on my personal Facebook Page. Alyssa, Tim, and I were overwhelmed with the response. When I went to my appointments in early December at Dana-Farber, my mom and dad took multiple trips to and from our car to deliver the many totes of toys. As my daughter, Alyssa. said, "It was a Christmas toy miracle."

Ten days before that very same Christmas of 2017, I fought an upper respiratory infection for over a week. In the middle of the night, I started coughing uncontrollably and had a bloody nose that would not stop. My husband called my transplant doctor and he told us to go to the Brigham and Women's emergency room.

My mom drove up in the middle of the night to stay with the kids. She barely stepped out of the car, and Tim and I left on our two-hour journey to the hospital. As expected, the emergency room was full of sick patients. With my fragile immune system, it was extremely concerning that I didn't have a private room. The next day, when I woke up from an exhaustion-induced nap, I heard my mom talking sternly with the doctors. She and Tim switched places so he could rest and prepare for work. For a few minutes I wasn't sure who was in charge of my care. I was moved to a corner room, the safest room for me.

Tests revealed that my platelet levels were extremely low. I received a transfusion, steroids to combat my raging graft-ver-sus-host symptoms, and an antibiotic for the upper respiratory infection. After a few days, I was finally released to go home. My first Christmas post-transplant might be a success after all.

News spread quickly through Facebook and word of mouth around town about my decorated sugar cookies. Tracy Kearcher for a Cure was being created. Baking and decorating personalized homemade sugar cookies became my creative outlet and ministry. A percentage of every sale went to the Leukemia & Lymphoma Society, just as I did with my crafts. Each month, more and more orders came in. I loved decorating the cookies. When I was baking, I forgot about my aches and pains.

Would leukemia come back tomorrow, or next month? I was too busy decorating to wonder or worry about the future. Before I knew it, my kids came home from school and it was time for myself and the grandparents to help them with homework and prepare dinner. Then it was bedtime routines and eventually falling into my own bed with Tim, feeling good about my productive day. I could also match my baking pace to my energy level. It was easy to work on the cookies for a bit and then finish them later, after a nap or a doctor's appointment. My mom and mother-in-law constantly teased me about the endless stream of dishes, but I could tell by the look in their eyes, they were thrilled I felt well enough to be baking.

# FIRST ANNIVERSARY

To celebrate my one-year transplant anniversary, we threw a huge party at Sonny's Place, a family entertainment center near our house. Many of the neighbors, friends, and other family members who helped us through our battle were invited. There was delicious food, fun games, fancy cocktails, a beautiful cake, and never-ending laughter. My son rode in a go-kart for the first time with me as the driver! With the wind whipping in my face, the sun gleaming off my skin, and the big smile emanating from my son next to me, I felt so alive! For the rest of my life, I will always cherish the way I felt that day: healthy, carefree, and deeply loved. WE DID IT! We were celebrating the fact that I had beat AML leukemia! I had stared death in the face and won.

I was free! No longer confined to my house as a medical prisoner, I could go to the Dollar Tree store, buy my own groceries, and browse through the racks at Target. Attending St. Luke's in person was something I had missed. One Sunday I spoke about my journey and thanked my fellow parishioners for all their support and encouragement. Seeing everyone at the coffee hour after Mass felt special. I also made a bountiful supply of my sugar cookies to share.

At the first follow-up appointment after the one-year post-transplant mark, another fun fact came out. Now I had the opportunity to receive a phlebotomy every other week. Because of the many blood transfusions during my chemotherapy treatments, there was too much iron in my blood. The options were a medicine with nasty side effects or getting poked again and sitting for an hour or two while a quart of blood was removed.

After the phlebotomy, I felt dizzy and nauseous for a day or two. This was done month after month for about a year, until my iron levels stayed in the normal range. Every other week my life stopped for a day or two as my body regained its equilibrium once again. Talking to other patients at the infusion center, some of them were gravely ill and not likely to win their fight. I was honored to befriend them and keep them company on their lonely journeys. My prayer for them was that they finish the remainder of their battle and fight well, which is the most any of us can hope for.

*"I have fought the good fight, I have finished the race, I have kept the faith"* (2 Timothy 4:7).

# THE NEVER-ENDING SQUALL

In some respects, my life post-leukemia is more challenging than when I was stuck in the hospital, fighting for my life for days on end. For one thing, I don't have a team of specialists addressing my new ailments and post-treatment side effects. Because I no longer look like a cancer victim, people can't tell that I'm damaged. "Slow down, Tracy," I constantly remind myself. My previous pace is no longer sustainable. Trying to achieve it will make me sick. Trust me, I've tried.

At the same time, the world moved on without me. When I emerged from Cancer Land, my children were two years older and each of my former hair clients had found new stylists. The process of figuring out who I was, post the storms, took time. The woman I used to be no longer existed. Things that were important to me felt foolish now.

The year I'm writing this book, I will be turning thirty-nine, and yet, I have more in common, physically and mentally, with people my parents' age. It's hard to relate to those in my own generation. While you won't hear me complain about my monthly "friend," I would love to get my period instead of relying on medications for hormone replacement. When someone complains about a bad day, I bite my tongue. While each of us experiences challenges differently, many have no idea how bad a day can be.

Many people seek advice for a friend or a family member undergoing treatment or recently diagnosed with cancer. This is a mixed blessing. I'm happy to share my experience and guide them through their personal war. However, every time I hear of another cancer diagnosis, my heart cracks open a bit more. I've been in the fray, and I know how dark and difficult the storm can be.

Leukemia broke me. Without tears and with a thyroid that no longer functions efficiently without medication, I am painfully aware of my weakness. Every inch of my skin is extremely dry and without prescriptions and daily routines, my body breaks down.

Faith is at the very top of my priority list each and every day. It has to be. Being broken is debilitating and exhausting. Looking at old pictures of my family and me, I don't recognize that girl in the picture. The sparkle in her eyes and her innocent smile are gone.

The first time I tried to explain it to Tim, when it was just the two of us curled on the couch, I said, "The girl in those pictures is dead." The Tracy Lynn Kearcher he married passed away the moment I received the acute myeloid leukemia diagnosis.

An invisible line was drawn with the diagnosis, separating me from everyone else. No one in the entire world experienced the exact details that I did. It was and is a very lonely and scary journey. I felt the separation most keenly watching those on the other side of it eat fresh vegetables and smell the crisp air outside of the hospital walls when I was stuck inside. They weren't subjected to endless prescriptions and being poked and prodded more times than they could count. Their lives didn't change overnight without any warning.

When my severe dry eyes were finally under control, I noticed my left eye's vision was increasingly blurry. It was harder to see. Because I thought my vision loss was related to the chronic dry eyes, I expected it to improve, but during a full vision screening, the doctor noticed nerve damage. High pressure caused it, and unfortunately, it was too late.

The result was an undiagnosed case of glaucoma. The factors increasing my odds of getting glaucoma included: LASIK performed in my early twenties, which means eye doctors have to guess my eye pressure, early-onset glaucoma in my family history, and all the steroids used throughout my treatments. I assumed like every other time in my past life that a prescription could fix it. This was not the case.

Today, I take eye drops to keep my eye pressure low and pray for my vision loss to remain slow. Glaucoma sometimes causes headaches and shadows. My best explanation is that I'm missing puzzle pieces from the field of vision in my left eye. The missing pieces of the puzzle leave black holes and can never be retrieved. Because there isn't a prescription or surgery to fix my vision, I cannot drive at night. I wish the burden of my limitations was not so hard on my family, especially with all the kids' activities as they get older.

While I mourn the loss of my healthy eyes, and sometimes fall into a pit of questioning why life is unfair, I remind myself, "Faith over fear, Tracy. Faith over fear." When I am scared and worried about my future vision, I focus on God's goodness and the tangible love of my family. Then there are the reminders from those around me of how my story and journey encourages and inspires them in their own lives.

Did you know "Chemo Brain" was a thing? After three rounds of chemo, it can be extremely hard for me to recall a name or a word. As a hairdresser I was fantastic at remembering clients' first names. In fact, former coworkers remarked on how often I called their client by name as well. Sometimes I even whispered their clients' names to them when I could tell they'd forgotten. That superpower is now gone. Word-retrieval issues are common with brain fog, aka Chemo Brain. I open my mouth for someone's name or a particular word and...nothing. It may sound silly, but it's an example of how my storms completely changed me, impacting every aspect of my body, mind, and ability. I'm not even forty yet.

Overall, my attitude is positive. I like it best when I'm busy with cookie orders, hanging out with my family, or working away in my home salon. Being occupied means the big black clouds of worry and fear blow farther into the distance. Helping my kids with their school-work and the constant movement of daily life keeps my mind and body active. It's the best treatment a post-transplant mom could ask for. I'm also noticing the need for activities for special-needs children in our area. As my kids grow older, I'm praying about opportunities to meet that need. I know what it's like to be lonely and isolated. No one should ever feel this way.

The power of prayer, faith, and a loving community are evident in my storm stories, and God brings countless opportunities to share my faith and message with others. I love that he is using my darkest days to bring light and hope to others. Restarting the St. Luke's Women's Guild in Ellington, Connecticut, with fellow church members and friends was invigorating; our mission is to build fellowship and a sense of community through spiritual, social, and charitable outreach in our community. Our goal is to touch as many lives as possible. It's growing in members and I couldn't be prouder of the group and its initiatives. Returning to teaching the Kindergarten Faith Formation class at church felt like a homecoming, a piece of the old Tracy I got to keep. It's fun being covered in paint and glue again and reminds me of the good old days with the Daisy troop.

The collateral damage of having leukemia affected my family too. There are certain songs and smells that bring them back to a particular day and experience during my stays at the hospital. If I happen to call my parents' house a little later than normal one night, I hear my mom catch her breath and can sense her heightened response of fear. Will another ball drop?

Going through these leukemia storms taught us all valuable life lessons. Every person has a unique story, all their own. Cancer affects people from every age, race, faith, and gender. We saw innocent little children undergoing treatments. With their bald little heads, jaundiced appearance, and a look of pure exhaustion on their tired little faces. Our hearts ached for them and their families.

Other times, I saw individuals fighting their battle alone. Time after time, day after day, they sat by themselves in the waiting room or while receiving treatment. There was no friend or family member with them, offering comfort. I couldn't imagine having to face it all by yourself. I thank God every day for the two caring and loving families in my life, one by birth and one by marriage.

My entire family takes pride in participating in cancer fundraisers and missions. Battling through the storms affected each of us profoundly and personally. My father, cousin, and her husband ride in the Smilow Closer to Free cancer bike ride each year. One year, my dad, cousin, and I were even featured in a video promotion for the ride before we participated in the forty-miler. I beamed when I saw the advertisement—at least all those hours of pain, fear, and anxiety was helping other cancer patients.

My mom, daughter, Tim, and I join in on the annual Relay for Life with our Team Holy Walkamolies. Thank you, Anna and Kim, for welcoming us onto your team. My daughter, Alyssa, created Beaded from the Heart, where she pieces together bracelets and necklaces. All proceeds from the beaded bracelets are donated to St. Jude's Children's Research Hospital. My sister continually shares our stem cell match success story for Be the Match.

Tracy Kearcher for a Cure is going strong with baking for special events and holidays. When someone ordered cookies for a fundraiser, she was hosting for a close friend going through his very own cancer battle, she asked how much for the cookies. Without hesitation, I replied, "They are on the house."

The Rise Above group in Ellington asked me to speak two different years about my experience with leukemia. The entire room full of teenagers was quiet and glued to my words. Each of these experiences was truly magical. At the time of typing this, Tracy Kearcher for a Cure has raised over $3000 for the Leukemia & Lymphoma Society, Closer to Free, and Relay for Life. My new life mission, for as long as God gives me strength and breath, is to spread leukemia awareness and fundraise.

There have been times over the years where I felt unworthy because I wasn't making a large paycheck. Now I remember that I have an extremely important job title: Cancer Survivor. My story gives hope to those suffering and I am uniquely equipped to offer aid and comfort to those going through a similar battle.

God blessed my family and I with remission and now my career goal is to support others to achieve remission too!

Each and every day I try to follow my mom's advice, the same words of wisdom she expressed as we drove away from Boston after my transplant, "Just take it one step at time."

This remains my mantra to this day. I focus on completing one fundraiser for cancer, one cookie order, and one follow-up doctor's appointment at a time. I turn up K-Love on my radio as the smell of cookies wafts through my house and dance to Unspoken's "Good Fight." If my kids are home, they join in, and if a stranger were to glance through the window, they might think we won the lottery with our impromptu dance party. In a way, we did.

Today and every day we celebrate the fact that I am alive, and we are committed to **Keep Living the Good Fight!**

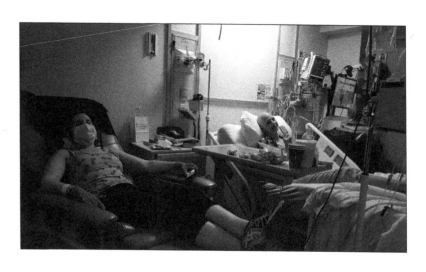

*Amanda and I after the transplant just hanging out*

*My dad, Cheryl and I in the Closer To Free Ride*

*Finally able to give Matthew a haircut again*

*Selling my cookies at the Ellington Farmer's Market*

*Decorating personalized elf cookies*

*My family in May of 2021 (the cutie on top is my godson)*

# THE RIPPLE EFFECT OF CANCER

Cancer not only impacts the body and life of the person diagnosed, it also changes the lives of those surrounding them. These are a few reflections of mine and my family members on the power of people within a community to make a difference. My hope is that they encourage and equip you with a glimpse of what the experience is like and practical ways to show your love and support to those going through a storm of their own.

**Thoughts from Amanda**

Tracy's younger sister and her perfect stem cell match

I don't think I have ever cried as much or as hard as I did the first few days after Tracy's diagnosis. Her skin had a gray color, and I will never forget the look of fear in her face or the anguish on my parents' faces. It's crazy how we spend so much time worrying about all the bad things that could happen, and even then, never consider something like this.

Growing up, I was the one with broken bones, hospital visits, and procedures, not Tracy. It happened so fast. She went from being mostly healthy her whole life, to having a stomach bug, a tooth infection, and then CANCER. I didn't realize it at the time, but I would never be the same again. When something like this happens, it changes one's perspective on reality. I realized, there's no way to know what life has in store for you. When a loved one goes through an experience like that, it makes you question why things happen the way they do.

Everything can change in an instant. For me, it was a text at seven a.m., "It's AML leukemia." I have never felt such a lack of control and vulnerability in my entire life. My whole world was hurting. I remember bits and pieces of conversations with my brother-in-law, my parents, and friends. I tried my best to be there for everyone grieving, but to be honest, I can't remember much of what I said, and I'm honestly not sure if it helped. We were all in shock and doing what we could to survive, knowing Tracy's prognosis was poor. When we found out that the chemotherapy was not effective and that doctors wanted to go ahead with the transplant, we were terrified.

I still remember the moment I found out I was a stem cell match. It was the first time in what felt like a very long time that I felt a bit of control. Hearing my sister's voice over the phone, sharing the good news, I could hear her smiling. It was amazing.

The process to set up the stem cell transplant was pretty easy. I was already in Boston frequently to visit. There was a physical and then a session with a therapist. She asked me how I felt about doing the transplant, knowing it might not work. Although I knew there was a possibility of failure, I knew it was our best option, the only option. At least I knew I did everything in my power to save her.

I was in Boston for a week during the donation and transplant. Taking medication for five days enabled my stem cells to separate from my bone marrow and enter my bloodstream. The medication process was simple but gave me a headache. My husband came up a few days before the donation. Unfortunately, I might actually have the world's smallest veins. The nurses had to put a PICC line in and then the donation took two days to complete. The last day was the worst of it for me. My husband pretty much carried me to the hospital.

My headache turned into a migraine, but I was not allowed to take medicine. That morning is a blur, but we got it done. Sitting in a wheelchair in my sister's dimly lit hospital room, I watched my stem cells slowly drain from the bag and travel into her port. We got it done.

It's still hard to believe the transplant was successful. The odds were against us and it blows my mind that we beat them. It's common for people who hear our story to say, "Wow, that's so nice of you." Others say, "You're so brave for doing that. I don't know if I could have done it."

Most of the time, I don't know what to say in response. I'm not the best at being the center of attention, and sometimes the praise people give me makes me uncomfortable. It's hard to view the situation as if there was a choice to be made. Wouldn't others have done the same for someone they loved?

My sister fought for her life for days on end. She battled cancer. She battled death. She was the one who suffered and sacrificed. I was given a rare opportunity that countless people have begged for. I had a chance to keep her alive. There was no choice. It was done the second I found out about the match, and I would do it a hundred more times if it meant keeping my family whole for one more day.

The thing about tragedy is that it brings out the best in people. It brought out an inner strength and resiliency in my sister, her husband, and my parents that I had never seen before. I didn't know it existed. There were also people who showered us with much love and kindness. It was remarkable.

I don't know why my sister got sick or why I was a perfect match, or even why the transplant worked. Who knows what the future will bring for us, but I am grateful every day that she is here with us. I feel blessed that we somehow got to keep her.

# THOUGHTS FROM TIM
## TRACY'S HUSBAND

Many of you reading this book have had family members, friends, coworkers and neighbors who've battled cancer. Some of you may have an evil disease today as you read Tracy's heart wrenching story of her battle. I've thought endlessly about what memories to add, hoping for some prolific and inspiring words. While that kind of miracle may not happen, another miracle a few years ago did take place. My beautiful, wonderful, and thoughtful wife was diagnosed with a gruesome strain of AML Leukemia and she defied all odds. Her strength, God's love, modern medicine, and the overwhelming support from everyone contributed to her survival. I don't know what I would do without her by my side. Or how our children would find their way through school and life without her love and guidance.

I became closer to God than I ever have during Tracy's battle. Listening to bands like Newsboys and Third Day or listening to a Joel Osteen podcast and not the ball game while driving back and forth from Boston helped me stay positive during this time of despair. As Tracy reminds us to live for today as none of us know what the future holds.

There are so many people that we'd like to thank. Neighbors who I barely knew showed up at our front door with a hot meal for our family, friends from out of state arriving at the hospital to visit Tracy, to community members organizing a fundraiser that had more support than we could have imagined. Part of me hesitated in putting pen to paper as it required reliving this experience. Tracy's battle is part of our everyday life. As I sit back and think about our life; I see our daughter saying prayers before meals, helping kids with disabilities and simply sharing smiles. Those small encounters that we take for granted can change someone's day and provide them with a ray of hope.

I wish I knew sooner that Tracy's condition was life threatening. The stomach discomfort and loss of energy she battled seemed, on the surface, to be a pesky virus or flu-like illness she was unable to shake. It was eerily reminiscent of a virus she battled two to three years earlier and which she fully recovered from.

Had we known sooner the true cause of her ailments was AML, we could have sought treatment sooner. Then Tracy may have been stronger when she entered round one of chemotherapy. Part of me also believes in fate. There was the dentist who directed us to Hartford Hospital and the oncologist at the hospital who recommended Dana Farber, instead of trying to treat Tracy himself. Then there was Dana Farber, who 'happened' to staff a world renowned Doctor, Joseph Antin. Had we made different decisions along the way, would the result have been the same?

# THOUGHTS FROM JOSEPH
## TRACY'S DAD

wish I'd known how long Tracy's battle for life was going to take. How we needed a crash course in medical/leukemia terminology to understand. There was so much to know as we tried to help Tracy and Tim make the most informed decisions.

As a parent, when your child is diagnosed, it's easy to feel helpless. Instead of feeling stuck, I focused on being there as much as Tracy needed me. Holding her hands tightly during the many painful bone marrow biopsies seemed to make a difference. Embracing her, cooling her many fevers with cold compresses, and giving her strength through prayer did too.

One of the surprising and miraculous experiences we had was when Marilyn and I met an angel. I truly believe God sent her to us in our time of despair. The very first time we went to see Tracy after her diagnosis, a complete stranger saw Marilyn and I devastated. She hugged us close and said with confidence, "God will get you through this. Put your worries in His hands."

The support and prayers from family and Marilyn's incredible network of friends were extremely helpful.

# THOUGHTS FROM MARILYN
## TRACY'S MOM

Facebook carried our message to people all across the country. A high school friend I hadn't spoken to in years made Tracy a prayer shawl. Friends and family reached out to help in every way possible. Friends scrubbed our home from ceiling to floors so Tracy could stay with us if need be. Another friend came three times a day to take care of our elderly dog, Maddie. Friends cooked meals and left them in the refrigerator so we had food when we arrived home every Friday night. The staff at Maple Hill Elementary School, where I was a first-grade teacher, always went above and beyond. They were constantly collecting money to support Joe and I. They also chipped in and got Alyssa and Matthew Easter goodies for their baskets. Some dear friends sent us prayers to pray as a family.

For other mothers out there who have a child battling an illness, my advice is be there for your child as much as possible. Surround them with your love, strength, and prayers. Remind them that God is with them always and to take it one day at a time.

# THOUGHTS FROM ALYSSA

Interview with Tracy's daughter, who was five
at the time of diagnosis

Thinking happy thoughts and praying to God helps you feel
better when your mom is very sick. Try to stay calm and take
deep breaths. Be sure to have your favorite stuffed animal with you
in bed every night to cuddle with. Foxy was with me every night
to keep the bad thoughts away. I missed my mom and was scared
she wouldn't come back home. I thought about how Mommy told
me she was with me all the time in my heart. I always remember
that saying.

# POST FROM A GOFUNDME FUNDRAISER

May 17, 2017

Tracy Kearcher is, by far, one of the best people I know. She and her husband Tim, moved to Ellington in the summer of 2015 with their two children, Alyssa, and Matthew. Tracy immediately became involved in the Ellington community through her church, MOMs Club, Center School PTO, and as a Girl Scout leader. As the mother of two school-aged children, juggling a career as the owner of Glitsy Girls Mobile Salon, along with various volunteer positions in ALL the above organizations, she quickly made friends and rooted herself in the Ellington community.

Shortly after the move, Tracy's son Matthew was diagnosed with mild autism. Along with this diagnosis, comes a long list of therapies and challenges. However, unlike many of us, she rarely complained. She was always positive and cheerful and looking on the bright side. She had recently took classes to learn more about Matthew's diagnosis and how to help him. Tracy thought that autism was going to be her biggest challenge in life. Unfortunately, life had a bigger battle in store just around the corner.

Throughout the month of March, Tracy had been experiencing some issues with an infected wisdom tooth that did not heal. One Saturday afternoon, when she could not bear the pain any longer, she went to the emergency room at Hartford Hospital. The medical staff ran some tests, and immediately admitted Tracy to the hospital. Within a matter of days, Tracy's life was turned upside down. On Monday morning, the doctor informed Tracy that she has acute myeloid leukemia, an aggressive form of leukemia. Tracy quickly started intense chemotherapy treatments. However, the first round of chemotherapy did not have the success that was hoped for. Tracy soon learned that she has a rare genetic mutation called inversion chromosome 3, which is associated with an extremely poor response to treatment. Tracy is currently undergoing her second round of chemotherapy at Dana Farber Institute in Boston. Following that, she hopes to have a bone marrow transplant. During this entire ordeal, months in the hospital, being separated from her children, Tracy has shown us all the true meaning of strength and grace. As a community organizer and volunteer, Tracy has always focused her attention on helping others. Now, she needs OUR help.

Our hearts reach out to this young family, and we want to help them with the financial strain that is quickly becoming a burden. While the Kearcher family battles AML, the cost of "normal" life goes on. Bills are the absolute last thing that should be on someone's mind while they fight for their life and undergo cancer treatment.

A group of friends from Center School, Girl Scouts and Ellington MOMs Club have teamed up! We hope to relieve expenses related to lodging, transportation, childcare, and healthcare/insurance copays and bills. We pray that, for Tracy, what began as a life-changing setback, will become a story of courage, thoughtful resolve, and ultimately, a return to good health. Let us help Tracy win her battle with leukemia.

# AUTHOR'S NOTES

My family and I experienced God's love throughout our journey in so many ways—from former clients, old neighbors, and friends of friends who donated dinners, money, or took time out from their busy lives to help my husband prepare our home for my return after my stem cell transplant.

The staff at Maple Hill Elementary School, who made the Easter bunny rock the year I was sick and made sure to always check in on my mom.

My husband's employers, the Antonacci Family, who made sure our family was never burdened financially.

Ellington staff and teachers who went above and beyond taking care of my babies when I couldn't be there for them.

The town of Ellington, who always kept me and my family in their prayers, and for that we will be eternally grateful!

The Enfield Stop & Shop Pharmacy went above and beyond helping my mother, in-laws, and Tim decipher how to take all my different medications and were always available to answer any questions we had.

Special thanks to:
Elle Salon & Spa in Cheshire, Connecticut
Jack and Allie's Children's Bookstore
Ellington Girl Scouts and the 2017 Ellington MOMS Club
Kloter's Ice Cream Barn
The Ellington Farmers Market
Erin Zumbo Photography Design

Deanne Welsh, founder of Unstoppable Writers, who gently shaped my words and thoughts, supporting the creation of my masterpiece.

God Bless You All!!

CPSIA information can be obtained
at www.ICGtesting.com
Printed in the USA
BVHW051202020921
615902BV00020B/898

9 781662 825217